Give Me Liberty!
An American History

Instructor's Manual and Test Bank

Volume One

ERIC FONER

GIVE ME LIBERTY!
An American History

INSTRUCTOR'S MANUAL
AND TEST BANK
BY

Valerie Adams
EMBRY-RIDDLE AERONAUTICAL UNIVERSITY

VOLUME ONE

W · W · NORTON & COMPANY · NEW YORK · LONDON

Printed in the United States of America

First Edition

ISBN 0-393-92551-X (pbk.)

W. W. Norton & Company, Inc., 500 Fifth Avenue, New York, N.Y. 10110
www.wwnorton.com

W. W. Norton & Company Ltd., Castle House, 75/76 Wells Street, London W1T 3QT

1 2 3 4 5 6 7 8 9 0

CONTENTS

PREFACE

This *Instructor's Manual and Test Bank* accompanies *Give Me Liberty! An American History* by Eric Foner. A groundbreaking textbook, its focus on freedom is a unifying theme that has much relevance for students today. The *Instructor's Manual and Test Bank* highlights that theme throughout, in an effort to help the instructor emphasize it in lectures and discussions.

This manual also helps instructors assess student mastery of the basic American history narrative. In today's political and diplomatic climate, public discussion often turns on issues of "freedom" and "liberty." The war on terrorism, which is being waged in part to protect American freedom, simultaneously impinges upon American freedom. Our conceptions of freedom have evolved over the centuries and Foner's text reminds us of our national struggle to broaden the definition so as not to exclude anyone. Freedom might entail property ownership, economic freedom, the freedom to speak out against the government, or the freedom to sit anywhere on a public bus. By tracing the constantly changing meanings of freedom in the context of an introductory American history, Foner has given us a textbook that is both timely and superbly written for the survey course. It is my hope that even seasoned veterans of the survey course find that the companion *Instructor's Manual and Test Bank* is useful for integrating the material in *Give Me Liberty!* into their current class curriculum.

The *Instructor's Manual* comprises the following elements for each chapter of the text: A chapter summary that offers a quick overview of the major themes and the topic of the *Voices of Freedom* primary-source insert. A detailed chapter outline follows, which can be used for lecture notes or PowerPoint presentations. The discussion of supplemental Web/visual material provides at least one video suggestion in addition to recommended Web sites that highlight the liberty theme. The discussions of supplemental print materials emphasize the most recent historical scholarship in monographs and journal articles. A series of classroom discussion questions concludes the *Instructor's Manual* portion.

The *Test Bank* includes some 2,000 matching, multiple-choice, true/false, short answer, and essay questions that assess student mastery of basic names, dates, and events. This volume also offers critical thinking, discussion, and essay questions that attempt to link various chapters and recurring themes. The intention of the volume is to balance pure memorization questions with application and critical thought questions, thereby providing a variety of exam questions to suit different needs and testing styles. For high-school teachers, the *Test Bank* complies with the Advance Placement format by offering five choices with each multiple-choice question.

This volume aims to help instructors new to the survey course with extensive chapter outlines, classroom discussion questions, and more than seventy test questions for each chapter. However, it also offers something for the experienced instructor by highlighting the freedom theme in the chapter summary, discussion, and essay questions and by suggesting new scholarship and Web sites.

My deepest appreciation and gratitude is extended to Steve Forman, senior editor at W. W. Norton, whose talent and vision made this volume infinitely stronger. I am also indebted to Sarah England at W. W. Norton for her patience and guidance through this project. Finally, I thank both Eric Foner and W. W. Norton for publishing a textbook that I hope inspires other instructors as it has inspired me and amplified my passion for the American history survey course.

Valerie Adams

CHAPTER 1 A New World

This chapter concentrates on the history of early European conquest of the Americas. European expansion by the Portuguese and Spanish, propelled by the search for African gold and a direct sea route to the Indian Ocean, is discussed in terms of European contact with African societies and through the voyages of Columbus. The chapter gives an overview of the Indian populations before European contact and their subsequent conquest by Spanish conquistadores. Spanish colonization is explored, with attention being given to justifications for conquest, the economy, forms of labor, and Spanish relations with Indians. Dominican priest Bartolomé de Las Casas is highlighted as a voice of freedom calling for better treatment for the Indians. North America is discussed next, with a focus again on the Indians and difference between the Indians and Europeans in terms of religion, perception of land, and gender roles. Europeans and Indians defined freedom differently, with the Europeans concluding that the concept was an alien notion for the Indians. Reasons for British interest in North America are explored, concluding that the unique history of England through the Magna Carta and its Civil War of the 1640s gave the English the belief that they were the world's guardians of liberty. As such, the English were destined to "free" the Americas from the hold of the Spanish. Freedom and the English are again highlighted in *Voices of Freedom,* where Henry Care discusses English liberties.

CHAPTER OUTLINE

I. Columbian Exchange

II. The Expansion of Europe
   A. Portugal and West Africa
      1. Caravelle, compass, and quadrant made travel along African coast possible for the Portuguese in the early fifteenth century

2. The search for African gold drove the early explorers
3. Portugal began colonizing Atlantic islands and established sugar plantations worked by slaves

B. Slavery and Africa
1. Slavery was already one form of labor in Africa before the Europeans came
2. Europeans traded textiles and guns for African slaves, which greatly disrupted African society
3. By the time Vasco da Gama sailed to India in 1498, Portugal had established a vast trading empire

C. The Voyages of Columbus
1. Christopher Columbus, an Italian, received financial support from King Ferdinand and Queen Isabella of Spain
2. Columbus landed on Hispaniola in 1492 and colonization began the next year
3. Amerigo Vespucci sailed along the coast of South America between 1498 and 1502, and the New World came to be called America based on Vespucci's name

III. Peoples of the Americas

A. The Settling of America
1. "Indians" settled the New World between 15,000 and 40,000 years ago, before the glaciers melted and submerged the land bridge between Asia and North America

B. Conquering the Americas
1. The native populations were significantly depleted through wars, enslavement, and diseases
2. The Spanish conquistadores Hernán Cortés and Francisco Pizarro conquered the Aztec and Inca empires respectively

IV. The Spanish Empire

A. Spain in America
1. Spain established a more stable government modeled after Spanish home rule
   a. Power flowed from the King to Council of the Indies to Viceroys to local officials
2. Gold and silver mines were the primary economies in Spanish America
   a. Mines were worked by Indians
   b. Many Spaniards came to the New World for easier social mobility
3. Spanish America evolved into a hybrid culture

B. Justifications for Conquest
1. To justify their claims to land that belonged to someone else, the Spanish relied on:
   a. cultural superiority
   b. violence

        c. missionaries
        d. the Pope
    2. National glory and religious mission went hand in hand, with the primary aim of the Spaniards to transform Indians into obedient, Catholic subjects of the Crown
  C. Spain and the Indians
    1. Bartolomé de Las Casas wrote about the injustices of Spanish rule toward the Indians
        a. He believed that "the entire human race is one," but supported African slavery
        b. His writings encouraged the 1542 New Laws, which forbade the enslavement of Indians
        c. Black Legend was an image put forth, in part, by Las Casas that Spain was an uniquely brutal and exploitive colonizer
  D. Spain in North America
    1. Spanish explorers migrated north in search of gold
        a. Florida was the first region within the present United States to be colonized by the Spanish
    2. Juan de Oñate led settlers into present-day New Mexcio
        a. Oñate's methods toward the native Acoma were brutal

V. The First North Americans
  A. Native American Societies
    1. Indians in North America did not resemble the empires of the Aztec or Inca civilizations
    2. Indians were very diverse and lived a variety of ways, some settling villages and some wandering as hunters
    3. By the fifteenth century some Indian tribes united into leagues or confederations in an effort to bring peace to local regions
  B. Religion, Land, and Gender
    1. Despite some similarities between Indian and European religious beliefs, Europeans still sought to "Christianize" the Indians
    2. The idea of private property was foreign to Indians
    3. Wealth and material goods were not sought after by Indians as compared to Europeans
    4. Many Indian societies were matrilineal
  C. Europeans and the Indians
    1. Europeans felt that Indians lacked genuine religion
    2. Europeans claimed that Indians did not "use" the land and thus had no claim to it
    3. Europeans viewed Indian men as weak and Indian women as mistreated
  D. Indians and Freedom
    1. Europeans concluded that the notion of "freedom" was alien to Indian societies

2. Indians were barbaric to the Europeans because they were *too* free
3. European understanding of freedom was based upon ideas of personal independence and the ownership of private property, foreign ideas to Indians

VI. England and the New World
 A. Unifying the English Nation
  1. England's stability in the sixteenth century was undermined by religious conflicts
  2. England's methods to subdue Ireland in the sixteenth and early seventeenth centuries established patterns that would be repeated in America
 B. England and New World Colonization
  1. The English crown issued charters for individuals to colonize America at their own expense, but they failed
  2. National glory, profit, and a missionary zeal motivated the English crown to settle America
   a. *A Discourse Concerning Western Planting* argued that settlement would strike a blow at England's enemy: Spain
   b. It was also argued that trade, not mineral wealth, would be the basis of England's empire
 C. The Social Crisis
  1. A worsening economy and the enclosure movement led to an increase of the poor and a social crisis
  2. Unruly poor were encouraged to leave England for the New World
 D. Masterless Men
  1. The English increasingly viewed America as a land where a man could control his own labor and thus gain independence, particularly through ownership of land

VII. The Freeborn Englishman
 A. Christian Freedom
  1. To embrace Christ was believed to provide a freedom from sin
  2. "Christian liberty" had no connection to later ideas of religious tolerance
 B. Freedom and Authority
  1. Obedience to law was another definition of freedom—law was liberty's "salvation"
  2. Under English law, a woman held very few rights and was submissive to her husband
  3. Freedom was a function of social class and as such a well-ordered society depended on obedience
   a. Liberty was often understood as formal privileges enjoyed by only a few
 C. The Rights of Englishmen
  1. The Magna Carta was signed by King John in 1215

   a. It identified a series of liberties, which barons found to be the most beneficial
2. The Magna Carta embodied the idea of English freedom
   a. habeas corpus
   b. the right to face one's accuser
   c. trial by jury
3. English Civil War of the 1640s illuminated debates about liberty and what it meant to be a "freeborn Englishman"

D. England's Debate over Freedom
1. The Levellers called for an even greater expansion of liberty, moving away from a definition based on social class
2. Diggers were another political group attempting to give freedom an economic underpinning
3. After the Civil War, there emerged a more general definition of freedom grounded in the common rights of all individuals within the English realm
   a. a belief in freedom as the common heritage of all Englishmen
   b. a belief that England was the world's guardian of liberty

SUGGESTED DISCUSSION QUESTIONS

- Evaluate "Gold, God, and Glory" as reasons for European conquest of the Americas. Did one outweigh another in motivating the Europeans? How were these reasons used to justify conquest? How genuine were they?
- The conquest of the New World by the Europeans resulted in the interaction between cultures. Discuss this interaction and how it affected both the Europeans and the Indians.
- Bartolomé de Las Casas was a voice of freedom for the Indians in Spanish America. Explain what motivated him to speak out. What kind of influence did he have on the Spanish? On the Indians? On African slaves? How can we tell that his understanding of freedom was limited?
- Describe the concept of the "Freeborn Englishman." What did it mean? How was it defined? Had that definition evolved?
- Private property is a uniquely European concept compared to the Indians' views toward land. Explain how private property played a pivotal role in both the Europeans' understanding of freedom and in their justification for conquest.

SUPPLEMENTAL WEB AND VISUAL RESOURCES

Columbian Exchange

www.nhc.rtp.nc.us/tserve/nattrans/ntecoindian/essays/columbian.htm

The National Humanities Center chronicles the Columbian Exchange with help from Alfred Crosby.

Conquistadores
www.pbs.org/conquistadors/
This is a two-volume PBS Home Video hosted by Michael Wood. Wood travels the routes that the Spanish conquistadores took in the sixteenth century. Cortez and the Pizarro brothers are highlighted.

1492: An Ongoing Voyage
www.ibiblio.org/expo/1492.exhibit/Intro.html
This is an exhibit hosted by the Library of Congress, providing a variety of resources and information about Columbus and the consequences of his voyage.

Images of Pre-Columbian America
newcrop.hort.purdue.edu/newcrop/history/lecture14/s_14.html
Hosted by Purdue, this site offers over fifty photographs of ancient artifacts.

Magna Carta
www.bl.uk/collections/treasures/magna.html
The British Library in London offers an image of the Magna Carta, an English translation, and valuable background information.

SUPPLEMENTAL PRINT RESOURCES

Axtell, James. "The Moral Dimensions of 1492." *The Historian* 56, no. 1 (1993): 17–28.

Crosby, Alfred. *The Columbian Exchange: Biological and Cultural Consequences of 1492.* New York: Greenwood Press, 1972.

Davis, David Brion. "Constructing Race: A Reflection." *William and Mary Quarterly* 54, no. 1 (1997): 7–18.

Greenblatt, Stephen. *Marvelous Possessions: The Wonder of the New World.* Chicago: University of Chicago Press, 1991.

Russell, Conrad. *The Causes of the English Civil War.* New York: Oxford University Press, 1990.

Townsend, Camilla. "Burying the White Gods: New Perspectives on the Conquest of Mexico." *The American Historical Review* 108, no. 3 (2003): 659–87.

TEST BANK

Matching

c 1. Christopher Columbus
f 2. Hernán Cortés
e 3. Adam Smith
h 4. Amerigo Vespucci

a. Claimed Brazil for Portugal in 1500
b. Englishman who settled Roanoke Island
c. Italian who sailed for Spain in 1492
d. Dominican priest who preached against Spanish rule

i	5. John Cabot	e. British economist who penned *The Wealth of Nations*
a	6. Pedro Cabral	f. Spanish conquistadore who conquered the Aztecs
d	7. Bartolomé de Las Casas	g. Described English government as a "qualified monarchy"
b	8. Sir Walter Raleigh	h. "America" was supposedly named for him
j	9. John Milton	i. First European to discover Newfoundland in 1497
g	10. Henry Care	j. Called for freedom of speech and the press in England

i	1. Columbian Exchange	a. society centered on the mother's family
h	2. coverture	b. document embodying English freedom
g	3. New Laws	c. a political movement favoring expanded liberties
f	4. mestizos	d. an ocean-going ship capable of great distances
j	5. Great League of Peace	e. large-scale farm owned by a Spanish landlord
c	6. Levellers	f. persons of mixed origins
b	7. Magna Carta	g. Spanish reform measures toward Indians
d	8. caravelle	h. a married woman surrendering her legal identity
a	9. matrilineal	i. transfer of goods and culture between New and Old Worlds
e	10. haciendas	j. confederation of five Iroquois tribes

Multiple Choice

1. Adam Smith recorded in 1776 that two events were the "two greatest and most important" in the history of mankind. What were they?
   *a. The discovery of America and the Portuguese sea route around Africa to Asia
   b. The discovery of America and the beginning of the slave trade
   c. The birth of mercantilism and the Portuguese sea route around Africa to Asia
   d. The beginning of the slave trade and the Portuguese sea route around Africa to Asia
   e. The discovery of America and the birth of mercantilism

2. The trans-Atlantic flow of people and goods such as corn, potatoes, horses, and sugar cane is called
   a. globalization
   *b. the Columbian Exchange

c. the Great Circuit
d. the Atlantic system
e. trade

3. What motivated the Portuguese to begin exploration to find a water route to the Orient?
a. To prove that the world was round
b. To spread Christianity by sailing for the Catholic Church
c. To establish land empires in India and China
*d. To eliminate the Italian and Muslim "middle men" in the spice trade
e. To search for gold

4. Of the approximately 10 million men, women, and children who came from the Old World to the New World between 1492 and 1820, how many were African slaves?
a. 2.4 million
b. 5.3 million
*c. 7.7 million
d. 9.1 million
e. none of the above

5. Which of the following statements about African slavery within Africa is false?
a. African slaves tended to be criminals, debtors, or captives in war
b. Slavery was one of several forms of labor in Africa
c. Slaves had well-defined rights and could possess property
d. The slave trade within Africa accelerated between 1450 and 1500
*e. Only men were taken for the slave trade

6. The "reconquista" was the reconquest of Spain from
a. the Jews
b. the British
c. the Protestants
*d. the Moors
e. the Aztecs

7. Indian population in Spanish America declined due to
a. enslavement
b. war
c. disease
*d. all of the above
e. none of the above

8. Alarmed by the destructiveness of the conquistadores, the Spanish crown replaced them with a more stable system of government headed by
*a. lawyers and bureaucrats
b. bishops of the Catholic Church

c. landed wealthy elite
d. elected local officials
e. businessmen

9. Which of the following statements about Spanish America is true?
*a. Over time, Spanish America evolved into a hybrid culture
b. Mestizos enjoyed much political freedom and held most of the high government positions
c. Spaniards outnumbered the Indian inhabitants within fifty years of settlement
d. The Catholic Church played only a minor role in Spanish America
e. Spanish America was very rural and had few urban centers

10. Spain justified her claim to land in the New World through all of the following except
a. believing that their culture was superior to the Indians
b. violence
c. a missionary zeal
d. a decree from the Pope
*e. a war against Britain

11. In 1542 Spain promulgated the New Laws, which
a. forbade African slavery
*b. forbade Indian slavery
c. forbade Catholic priests from speaking out against Spanish policy
d. divided the New World between the Spanish and Portuguese
e. replaced the outdated Old Laws

12. The Black Legend described
a. the Aztecs' view of Cortés
b. English pirates along the African coast
*c. Spain as an uniquely brutal colonizer
d. Portugal as a vast trading empire
e. Indians as savages

13. Which of the following statements about the Indians of North America is false?
a. Indians were very diverse
b. The idea of private property was foreign to Indians
c. Many Indian societies were matrilineal
d. Indians did not covet wealth and material goods like the Europeans did
*e. Indians lacked genuine religion

14. The English and Indians did not understand the concept of freedom the same way because the English based freedom upon
*a. land
b. Christianity

c. material wealth
d. a patriarchal society
e. a written code of law

15. England's methods to subdue which group in the sixteenth century established patterns that would be repeated in North America?
a. Scottish
b. Welsh
*c. Irish
d. African slaves in the West Indies
e. none of the above

16. What motivated the English crown to colonize America?
a. national glory
b. to strike a blow against Spain
c. to establish a trading empire
*d. all of the above
e. none of the above

17. What did some believe to be liberty's "salvation"?
a. faith
b. money
c. private property
*d. the law
e. a hierarchal society

18. What idea did the Magna Carta not embody?
a. habeas corpus
*b. religious freedom
c. trial by jury
d. the right to face one's accuser
e. none of the above

19. The Levellers and Diggers were
*a. political groups
b. labor groups
c. conquistadores
d. names of British ships
e. Indian tribes

20. A consequence of the English Civil War of the 1640s was
*a. belief that England was the world's guardian of liberty
b. increased slave trading
c. the establishment of Plymouth Colony
d. the signing of the Magna Carta
e. war between Spain and England

True or False

T 1. Portuguese seafarers initially hoped to locate African gold.

F 2. African society did not practice slavery before Europeans came.

T 3. Europeans mostly traded textiles and guns for African slaves.

F 4. Columbus was Spanish.

F 5. Columbus first sailed to modern-day Venezuela.

T 6. The catastrophic decline in the native populations in Spanish America was mostly due to the fact that they were not immune to European diseases.

T 7. Cortés conquered the capital city of the Aztec empire with an army of over one thousand men.

T 8. By 1550, the Spanish empire in the New World exceeded the ancient Roman Empire in size.

F 9. In British America, unlike other New World empires, Indians performed most of the labor in the colonies.

T 10. Peninsulares stood atop the social hierarchy in Spanish America.

T 11. Spain insisted that the primary goal of colonization was to save the Indians from heathenism.

F 12. The Spanish aim was to exterminate or remove the Indians from the New World.

T 13. The Indians of North America believed that land was a common resource and the basis of economic life.

F 14. Early modern England was an egalitarian society where many enjoyed both economic wealth and political power.

T 15. *A Discourse Concerning Western Planting* argued that English settlement of North America would strike a blow against Spain.

T 16. The English increasingly viewed America as a land where a man could control his own labor and thus gain independence.

F 17. "Christian liberty" was the basis for religious toleration.

F 18. Under English law, women held many legal rights and privileges.

T 19. After the English Civil War it was generally believed that freedom was the common heritage of all Englishmen.

T 20. Henry Care believed that the English system of government was the best in the world.

Short Answer

Identify and give the historical significance of each of the following terms, events, and people in a paragraph or two.

1. Conquistadores
2. "Freeborn Englishman"
3. Private Property
4. African slave trade
5. Columbian Exchange
6. The Black Legend
7. English Civil War
8. Magna Carta
9. Henry Care
10. Bartolomé de Las Casas

Essay Questions

1. Explain as thoroughly as you can how the slave trade affected African society.
2. One Spanish official remarked that "the maxim of the conqueror must be to settle." Explain what you think he meant by this statement. Illustrate the various ways conquerors settled the New World, commenting on what worked, what did not work, and consequences of those methods.
3. Explain the chapter's title: "A New World." What was "new"? Is it an appropriate term? Does perspective play a role in calling the Americas "new"? Be sure to comment on whether or not freedom was "new" in this "New World."
4. Compare Indian society with that of the Europeans. What differences were there? Similarities? Be sure to include in your analysis ideas about religion, land, and gender roles, as well as notions about freedom.
5. Compare Spanish America and British America. Discuss reasons for settlement, attitudes toward Indians, forms of labor, major economies, role of religion, and systems of government. How was freedom defined in the two colonies? What liberties were extended and to whom?
6. Explain as thoroughly as you can what allowed Spain and Britain to claim possession of lands that "belonged to someone else." What arguments were made? How were their actions justified? How did the definition of freedom play a role?
7. Henry Care argued that the Constitution of the English government was the best in the world. Explain why he believed that. Was he right?
8. How had the concept of the English freeman developed through the centuries? What had defined freedom and to whom were liberties granted? How and why had those definitions changed over the centuries?

CHAPTER 2 American Beginnings, 1607–1650

This chapter concentrates on the early history of the Chesapeake and New England colonies, between 1607 and 1650. It begins by exploring who was emigrating to North America and for what reasons. Land is discussed as a basis of liberty and the colonists' attitudes towards Indian land is examined in depth. Indentured servitude versus slave labor is a theme repeated throughout the chapter. It examines settlement of the Chesapeake region, identifying tobacco as the area's "gold," and how that labor-intensive crop intensified the desirability of slave labor. Lines between slavery and freedom are discussed, explaining that such lines were ambiguous in the seventeenth century and that race and racism were new concepts to the late seventeenth century. Religion and freedom are common themes in this chapter, relevant to the establishment of Maryland, Massachusetts, and Rhode Island. The Puritan distinction between moral liberty and religious freedom plays a significant role in the banishment of Roger Williams and Anne Hutchinson from the Massachusetts colony. Puritanism and liberty are highlighted in *Voices of Freedom*, with an excerpt from a speech given by John Winthrop. The chapter examines Puritan society and compares it with the Chesapeake colonies. Gender roles are explored in each section. The chapter concludes with a look at the New England economy, noting the irony in that the growth of the economy was in part due to the Puritans' work ethic, but that such economic growth was at the same time weakening their power and influence.

CHAPTER OUTLINE

I. Jamestown

II. The Coming of the English
  A. English Colonists
    1. Sustained immigration was vital for the settlement's survival

2. Between 1607 and 1700, a little over half-a-million persons left England
    a. They settled in Ireland, the West Indies, and North America
    b. The majority in North America were young, single men from the bottom rungs of English society

B. Indentured Servants
1. Two-thirds of English settlers came to North America as indentured servants
2. Indentured servants did not enjoy any liberties while under contract

C. Land and Liberty
1. Land was the basis of liberty

D. Englishmen and Indians
1. The English were chiefly interested in displacing the Indians and settling on their land
2. Most colonial authorities in practice recognized Indians' title to land based on occupancy
3. The seventeenth century was marked by recurrent warfare between colonists and Indians
    a. Wars gave the English a heightened sense of superiority

E. Changes in Indian Life
1. English goods were eagerly integrated into Indian life
2. Over time, those European goods changed Indian farming, hunting, and cooking practices
    a. Exchanges with Europeans stimulated warfare among Indian tribes
3. As the English sought to reshape Indian society and culture, their practices only undermined traditional Indian society

III. Settling the Chesapeake

A. The Jamestown Colony
1. Settlement and survival were questionable in the colony's early history because of high death rates, frequent changes in leadership, inadequate supplies from England, and placing gold before farming
2. By 1616, about 80 percent of the immigrants who had arrived in the first decade were dead
3. John Smith began to get the colony on its feet and new policies were adopted in 1618 so that the colony could survive:
    a. headright system
    b. a charter of grants and liberties
    c. slavery; the first slaves arrived in 1619

B. Powhatan's World
1. Powhatan, the leader of thirty tribes near Jamestown, eagerly traded with the English
2. English-Indian relations were mostly peaceful initially
    a. Pocahontas married John Rolfe in 1614, symbolizing Anglo-Indian harmony

C. The Uprising of 1622
   1. Once the English decided on a permanent colony instead of merely a trading post, conflict was inevitable
      a. Opechancanough led an attack on Virginia's settlers in 1622
   2. The English forced the Indians to recognize their subordination to the government at Jamestown and moved them onto reservations
   3. The Virginia Company surrendered its charter to the crown in 1624
D. A Tobacco Colony
   1. Tobacco was Virginia's "gold" and its production reached 30 million pounds by the 1680s
   2. The expansion of tobacco led to an increased demand for field labor
E. Women and the Family
   1. Virginian societies lacked a stable family life
   2. Social conditions opened the door to roles women rarely assumed in England
F. The Maryland Experiment
   1. Maryland was established in 1632 as a proprietary colony under Cecilius Calvert
   2. Calvert imagined Maryland as a feudal domain, but one that would act as a place of refuge for persecuted Catholics
   3. Although Maryland had a high death rate, it seemed to have offered servants greater opportunity for land ownership than Virginia
   4. Religious and political battles emerged and Maryland was on the verge of total anarchy in the 1640s
   5. In 1649, the Act Concerning Religion was adopted, a milestone in the history of religious freedom in colonial America

IV. Origins of American Slavery
A. Englishmen and Africans
   1. The spread of tobacco led settlers to turn to slavery, which offered many advantages over indentured servants
   2. In the early to mid seventeenth century, the concepts of race and racism had not fully developed
   3. Africans were seen as alien in their color, religion, and social practices
B. Slavery in History
   1. Although slavery has a long history, slavery in the North America was markedly different
   2. Slavery developed slowly in the New World because slaves were expensive and their death rate was high in the seventeenth century
C. Slavery and the Law
   1. The line between slavery and freedom was more permeable in the seventeenth century than it would later become
      a. Some free blacks were allowed to sue and testify in court
      b. Anthony Johnson arrived as a slave but became a slave-owning plantation owner

2. It was not until the 1660s that the laws of Virginia and Maryland explicitly referred to slavery
3. A Virginia law of 1662 provided that in the case of a child who had one free and one enslaved parent, the status of the offspring followed that of the mother
4. In 1667 the Virginia House of Burgesses decreed that religious conversion did not release a slave from bondage

D. A Slave Society
1. A number of factors made slave labor very attractive to English settlers by the end of the seventeenth century, and slavery began to supplant indentured servitude between 1680 and 1700
2. By the early eighteenth century, Virginia had transformed from a society with slaves to a slave society
    a. In 1705, the House of Burgesses enacted strict slave codes

E. Notions of Freedom
1. From the start of American slavery, blacks ran away and desired freedom
2. Settlers were well aware that the desire for freedom could ignite the slaves to rebel

V. The New England Way

A. The Rise of Puritanism
1. Puritanism emerged from the Protestant Reformation in England
    a. Puritans believed that the Church of England retained too many elements of Catholicism
2. Puritans considered religious belief a complex and demanding matter, urging believers to seek the truth by reading the Bible and listening to sermons
    a. Puritans followed the teachings of John Calvin
3. Many Puritans immigrated to the New World in hopes of establishing a Bible Commonwealth that would eventually influence England
4. Puritans were governed by a "moral liberty"

B. The Pilgrims at Plymouth
1. Pilgrims sailed in 1620 to Cape Cod aboard the *Mayflower*
    a. Adult men signed the Mayflower Compact before going ashore
2. Squanto provided valuable help to the Pilgrims and the first Thanksgiving was celebrated in 1621

C. The Great Migration
1. The Massachusetts Bay Company was charted in 1629 by London merchants wanting to further the Puritan cause and to turn a profit from trade with the Indians
2. New England settlement was very different compared to the Chesapeake colonies
    a. New England had a more equal balance of men and women
    b. New England enjoyed a longer life expectancy

    c. New England had more families
    d. New England enjoyed a healthier climate
- D. The Puritan Family
    1. Puritans reproduced the family structure of England with men at the head of the household
    2. Women were allowed full church membership and divorce was legal, but a woman was expected to obey her husband fully
    3. Puritans believed that a woman achieved genuine freedom by fulfilling her prescribed social role and embracing subjection to her husband's authority
- E. Government and Society in Massachusetts
    1. Massachusetts was organized into self-governing towns
        a. Each town had a Congregational church and a school
        b. To train an educated ministry, Harvard College was established in 1636
    2. The freemen of Massachusetts elected their governor
    3. Church government was decentralized
        a. Full church membership was required to vote in colony-wide elections
        b. Church and colonial government were intricately linked
- F. Puritan Liberties
    1. Puritans defined liberties by social rank, producing a rigid hierarchical society justified by God's will
    2. The Body of Liberties affirmed the rights of free speech and assembly and equal protection for all

VI. New England Divided

- A. Roger Williams
    1. A young Puritan minister, Williams preached that any citizen ought to be free to practice whatever form of religion he chose
    2. Williams believed that it was essential to separate church and state
    3. Williams was banished from Massachusetts in 1636 and he established Rhode Island
    4. Rhode Island was truly a beacon of religious freedom and democratic government
    5. Other former members of Massachusetts included New Haven and Hartford, which joined to become the colony of Connecticut in 1662
- B. The Trials of Anne Hutchinson
    1. Hutchinson was a well-educated, articulate woman who charged that nearly all the ministers in Massachusetts were guilt of faulty preaching
    2. Hutchinson was placed on trial in 1637 for sedition
        a. On trial she spoke of divine revelations
        b. She and her followers were banished

3. As seen with Williams and Hutchinson, Puritan New England was a place of religious persecution
   a. Quakers were hanged in Massachusetts
   b. Religious tolerance violated "moral liberty"

C. Puritans and Indians
1. Colonial leaders had differing opinions about the English right to claim Indian land
2. To New England's leaders, the Indians represented both savagery and temptation
   a. The Connecticut General court set a penalty for anyone who chose to live with the Indians
   b. No real attempt to convert the Indians was made by the Puritans in the first two decades
3. Colonists warred against the Pequots in 1637, exterminating the tribe

VII. The New England Economy

A. Merchants
1. Most migrants were textile craftsmen and farmers
2. Fishing and timber were exported, but the economy centered on family farms
3. Per capita wealth was equally distributed compared to the Chesapeake
4. A powerful merchant class rose up, which occasionally clashed with the church

B. The Half-Way Covenant
1. By 1650, the church had to deal with the third generation of the Great Migration
2. In 1662, the Half-Way Covenant was a compromise for the grandchildren of the Great Migration, granting half-way membership into the church

SUGGESTED DISCUSSION QUESTIONS

- Why was the Jamestown Colony unstable and survival questionable? Who settled there? What were their goals? What were their relations like with the Indians?
- Explain the religious attitudes held in Maryland. How did they compare to Rhode Island? The Puritans? How was religious freedom defined in each colony?
- What were the pros and cons of indentured servitude for the employer? Pros and cons of slavery? Compare the two labor systems, explaining why one was preferred over the other. What freedoms did each have?
- What were the differences between the Pilgrims and the Puritans? Compare Plymouth colony with the Massachusetts Bay colony.

- How were Puritan women expected to achieve genuine freedom?
- Explain how Roger Williams and Anne Hutchinson showed how the Puritan belief in each individual's ability to interpret the Bible could easily lead to criticism of the religious establishment.

SUPPLEMENTAL WEB AND VISUAL RESOURCES

Africans in America
www.pbs.org/wgbh/aia/home.html
Africans in America is a four-part PBS video about America's journey through slavery. Part I: "The Terrible Transformation, 1450–1750."

Jamestown Rediscovery
www.apva.org/jr.html
The Association for the Preservation of Virginia Antiquities homepage for Jamestown. Provides history of the settlement and archeological information.

Mayflower History
www.mayflowerhistory.com
Homepage for a site that provides historical facts about the *Mayflower* and full-text primary sources of books and letters written by passengers of the *Mayflower*.

The 1629 Charter of Massachusetts Bay
www.law.ou.edu/hist/massbay.html
The University of Oklahoma Law Center has posted the document of the charter of the Massachusetts Bay Company.

Chesapeake Colonies
www.mariner.org/chesapeakebay/colonial/col003.html
The Mariner's Museum's Web site contains the history of the various colonies in the Chesapeake Bay area.

Pocahontas
store.aetv.com/
This A&E biography titled "Pocahontas: Her True Story," is a 50-minute video on the remarkable life of the wife of John Smith.

SUPPLEMENTAL PRINT RESOURCES

Davis, David Brion. "Constructing Race: A Reflection." *William and Mary Quarterly* 54, no. 1 (1997): 7–18.

Irwin, Raymond. "Cast out from the 'City upon a Hill': Antinomianism Exiles in Rhode Island, 1638–1650." *Rhode Island History* 52, no. 1 (1994): 2–19.

Morgan, Edmund. *The Puritan Dilemma: The Story of John Winthrop*. New York: Longman, 1999.

Nicholson, Bradley. "Legal Borrowing and the Origins of Slave Law in the British Colonies." *American Journal of Legal History* 38, no. 1 (1994): 38–51.

Quitt, Martin. "Trade and Accumulation at Jamestown, 1607–1609: The Limits of Understanding." *William and Mary Quarterly* 52, no. 2 (1995): 227–58.

Saxton, Martha. "Bearing the Burden? Puritan Wives." *History Today* (1994): 28–33.

TEST BANK

Matching

h	1. Squanto	a. proprietor of Maryland
f	2. John Smith	b. wife of John Rolfe
g	3. Anne Hutchinson	c. Pilgrim leader
d	4. Powhatan	d. leader of Indians near Jamestown
i	5. John Calvin	e. governor of Massachusetts
j	6. Roger Williams	f. settler of Jamestown
a	7. Cecilius Calvert	g. was denounced for Antinomianism
e	8. John Winthrop	h. Indian who helped the Pilgrims
c	9. William Bradford	i. preached about the elect and the damned
b	10. Pocahontas	j. established Rhode Island

e	1. Virginia Company	a. gave 5–7 years of service for passage to America
a	2. indentured servant	b. believed the spirit of God dwelled in all persons
i	3. Puritans	c. monies or land given to indentured servants
h	4. tobacco	d. first elected assembly in colonial America
f	5. Mayflower Compact	e. charter company that established Jamestown
j	6. headright system	f. first written frame of government in British America
b	7. Quakers	g. a compromise for the descendants of the Great Migration
c	8. freedom dues	h. primary economy of the Chesapeake colonies
d	9. House of Burgesses	i. argued the Church of England was still too Catholic
g	10. Half-Way Covenant	j. giving fifty acres to anyone who paid his own passage

Multiple Choice

1. Despite the dangers, many English were drawn to North America because
   a. economic conditions in England were bad
   b. there was a constant demand for cheap labor in North America
   c. it was a natural extension of the migration at home of an increasingly mobile English population
   d. land was believed to be plentiful in North America
   *e. all of the above

2. Indentured servants
   *a. could be bought and sold
   b. could marry whomever they pleased without permission from their owner
   c. could not be subjected to physical punishments
   d. could not have their contract extended if they became pregnant
   e. were able to nullify their labor obligation by the courts

3. What did English settlers believe was the basis of liberty?
   a. freedom
   *b. land
   c. citizenship
   d. belief in God
   e. economic independence

4. The English were chiefly interested in
   a. organizing Indian labor
   b. making the Indians subjects of the Crown
   c. merging English communities with Indian communities
   *d. displacing Indians from their land
   e. converting Indians to Christians

5. Why was the survival of Jamestown initially questionable?
   a. high death rate of its settlers
   b. leadership changed repeatedly
   c. settlers were more concerned with seeking a quick profit
   d. supplies from England were inadequate
   *e. all of the above

6. The marriage between John Rolfe and Pocahontas did what?
   a. brought unrest and conflict between the English and the Indians
   b. split the church
   *c. symbolized Anglo-Indian harmony and missionary success
   d. marked the beginnings of many ethnically mixed marriages between Indians and the English
   e. caused King James I to denounce John Rolfe

7. It can be argued that conflict between the English and local Indians became inevitable when what occurred?
   *a. when the English decided to establish a permanent colony, not just a trading post
   b. when Pocahontas married John Rolfe
   c. when John Smith established Jamestown
   d. when Opechancanough led an attack against the Virginian settlers
   e. none of the above

8. Out of the 6,000 persons sent to Virginia via the Virginia Company, what was the approximate population of the settlement in 1624 when it surrendered its charter to the English Crown?
   a. 7,000
   b. 6,000
   c. 4,000
   d. 3,000
   *e. 1,000

9. What was Virginia's "gold," that ensured its survival and prosperity?
   a. cotton
   b. fur
   *c. tobacco
   d. indigo
   e. sugar

10. To entice settlers to Virginia, the Virginia Company established the headright system, which
    a. granted religious freedom
    *b. provided land to settlers who paid their own passage
    c. brought slavery to the colony
    d. promised every single man a bride
    e. enslaved Indians

11. Which statement about women in the early Virginia colony is false?
    a. Women mostly came to Virginia as indentured servants
    b. Some women took advantage of their legal status as "femme sole"
    *c. Women composed about half the white population
    d. Women often married at a relatively late age — mid-20s
    e. There was a high death rate among women

12. Which colony adopted the Act Concerning Religion in 1649, which institutionalized the principle of toleration?
    a. Virginia
    *b. Maryland
    c. Massachusetts
    d. Rhode Island
    e. Connecticut

13. English Puritans
    a. were loyal to Charles I
    *b. believed that the Church of England still closely resembled the Catholic Church in its rituals
    c. fled to France for religious freedom before coming to America
    d. followed the teachings of Protestant theologian Martin Luther
    e. believed in the separation of church and state

14. The Mayflower Compact established
    a. religious toleration and freedom
    b. the right to emigrate to America
    c. a charter company
    *d. a civil government for the colony
    e. relations with the local Indians

15. Puritan women
    a. could not legally divorce
    b. were not allowed full church membership
    *c. achieved freedom by embracing subjection to their husbands' authority
    d. could become ministers
    e. married late in life

16. Puritans defined liberty through
    a. social rank
    b. God
    c. the "Book of Liberties"
    d. custom
    *e. all of the above

17. In Massachusetts, "freeman" status was granted to adult males who
    a. owned land, regardless of church standing
    b. had served their term as an indentured servant
    c. were freed slaves
    *d. were landowning church members
    e. voted

18. Rhode Island
    *a. had no established church
    b. required all male citizens to attend church
    c. elected its assembly and governor only every four years
    d. had no mechanism for town meetings
    e. was established by Anne Hutchinson

19. New England's economy was based on
    a. tobacco
    b. sugar
    *c. trade

d. banking
e. fishing

20. In contrast to life in the Chesapeake region, life in New England
*a. was more family oriented
b. was not as structured
c. was not characterized as a deeply religious area
d. saw more independent roles for women
e. centered upon an economy based on one cash crop

True or False

T 1. Jamestown was originally settled by just men.

F 2. Disease killed many Indians, but European settlers were not affected by disease.

T 3. Nearly two-thirds of English settlers came as indentured servants.

T 4. English settlers believed land was the basis of liberty.

F 5. Snowshoes and canoes were English and brought over to North America where the Indians adopted their use.

T 6. Indians traded mostly furs and animal skins for European goods.

F 7. Growing connections with Europeans lessened warfare among Indian tribes.

T 8. Early settlers of Jamestown preferred gold to farming.

T 9. Treatment of the Indians by members of the Virginia colony was influenced in part by Las Casas's condemnation of Spanish behavior.

F 10. The Virginia Company accomplished its goals for the company and for its settlers.

T 11. Believing that tobacco was harmful to one's health, King James I warned against its use.

F 12. Roger Williams imagined Rhode Island as a feudal domain.

T 13. Freedom dues in Maryland included fifty acres of land.

F 14. Even Jewish people enjoyed religious freedom under the Act Concerning Religion.

T 15. Concepts of race and racism had not fully developed in the early seventeenth century.

F 16. Puritans believed that the Church of England was in no need of reform.

F 17. The Pilgrims intended to set sail for Cape Cod in 1620.

F 18. Like the Virginia Company, the settlers of Massachusetts were mostly families.

T 19. Puritans relied upon and deeply valued education.

T 20. Religious toleration violated the Puritan understanding of "moral liberty."

Short Answer

Identify and give the historical significance of each of the following terms, events, and people in a paragraph or two.

1. indentured servants
2. Puritans
3. "moral" versus "natural" liberty
4. land and liberty
5. Act Concerning Religion
6. Roger Williams
7. Virginia Company
8. tobacco
9. Anne Hutchinson
10. headright system

Essay Questions

1. Explain as thoroughly as you can what John Smith meant when he remarked that "No man will go from [England] to have less freedom."

2. Many degrees of freedom coexisted in seventeenth-century North America. Discuss the various definitions of freedom. Be sure to include slaves, indentured servants, women, Indians, property owners, and Puritans in your discussion. Identify any similarities and differences among these different versions of freedom.

3. Explain the reasons behind the various conflicts between the English and the Indians. How does perception of land and liberty fit into the story? How does trade play a part? Why and when did the Indians attack first? Why and when did the settlers attack?

4. Early British North America witnessed the use of various labor systems. Fully describe those systems, comparing and contrasting, and analyze why slavery was slow to come to British North America. What liberties were extended to those whose labor was not free?

5. The line between slavery and freedom was more permeable in the seventeenth century than it would later become. Explain how slavery was treated in the seventeenth century by discussing the law, customs, and liberties extended to slaves. What had to happen for the line between slavery and freedom to harden?

6. John Winthrop distinguished between "natural" and "moral" liberty. What was the difference? How did moral liberty work and how did Puritans define liberty and freedom? Discuss the restrictions of moral liberty and the consequences as illustrated by Roger Williams and Anne Hutchinson. Be sure to address Winthrop's speech in the *Voices of Freedom* box.

7. Compare the Chesapeake and New England colonies. Explore the various reasons for the colonists' emigrating to the New World, their economies, gender roles, demographics, religion, and relations with the Indians. Which pattern of settlement is more representative of American development after the seventeenth century?

8. Both religious freedom and the separation of church and state are taken for granted today. In seventeenth century British America, freedom and religion did not necessarily go hand in hand, for many believed that the church ought to influence the state. Describe the varying degrees of religious freedom practiced in the colonies. Why were some colonies seemingly devoid of religion? Why were the Puritans intent upon religious persecution? What were the limitations placed in Maryland? Describe too how the colonies viewed church and state. What were the reasons to unite the two? Why did some argue that they should be separated?

CHAPTER 3 Crisis and Expansion: North American Colonies, 1650–1750

This chapter concentrates on the reasons behind a colonial crisis and the resulting expansion of liberty. The chapter begins with a description of the growing North American colonies by the Dutch and French. Liberty plays a central role in the New Netherlands and offers a unique comparison to British America. The French empire is also different from British America, particularly in its relationships with the Indians. The chapter moves on to explore the growth of the English commercial empire through mercantilism, slavery, and the establishment of colonies in New York, Carolina, and Pennsylvania. William Penn, the proprietor of Pennsylvania, is highlighted in the *Voices of Freedom* box, as his "holy experiment" held many liberties for all of its inhabitants. A colonial crisis is described through a series of local conflicts such as Bacon's Rebellion, King Philip's War, and the Salem Witch Trials. After the Glorious Revolution, American colonists began to believe that they were entitled to certain liberties. The chapter concludes with a broad look at eighteenth-century colonial society, which was becoming increasingly diverse and consumer driven.

CHAPTER OUTLINE

I. Pueblo Revolt of 1680
   A. Inquisition
      1. Successful Pueblo rebellion against the Spanish in 1680
      2. Spain learned a lesson in tolerance

II. Empires in Conflict
   A. The Dutch Empire
      1. Henry Hudson claimed New York for the Netherlands in 1609
      2. By the early seventeenth century, the Netherlands was a formidable trading empire and banking center
      3. The Dutch came to North America to trade, not to conquer

4. Dutch authorities recognized Indian sovereignty over the land and forbade settlement in any area until it had been purchased

B. Freedom in New Netherland
   1. New Netherland was not governed democratically
   2. Slaves enjoyed half-freedoms
   3. Women enjoyed liberties not bestowed upon English women, including retaining their legal identity after marriage
   4. Religious freedoms were extensive, with toleration extended to Catholics and Jews
   5. Large estates were offered to patroons, who could run their estate like a medieval lord
      a. Kiliaen Van Rensselaer

C. French Colonization
   1. By the late seventeenth century, France had claims arching from St. Lawrence to New Orleans
   2. Migration to New France was largely by men, with fewer than 20 percent women and only 250 complete families
   3. The French government feared that significant emigration to the New World would undermine France's role as a European great power

D. New France and the Indians
   1. Since New France relied upon fur trade with the Indians, the French tried to develop friendly relations with the local Indians
      a. The result was some of the most enduring alliances between Indians and settlers in colonial North America
   2. Contact with the French brought devastating disease to the Indians
   3. The French were much more accepting of Indians into colonial society than the British

III. The Expansion of England's Empire

A. The Mercantilist System
   1. England attempted to regulate its economy to ensure wealth and national power
      a. Commerce was the foundation of empire, not territorial plunder
   2. The Navigation Acts required colonial products to be transported in English ships and sold at English ports

B. The Conquest of New York
   1. The New Netherlands was seized in 1664 during an Anglo-Dutch war
   2. The terms of Dutch surrender guaranteed some freedoms and liberties, but reversed others
   3. The Duke of York governed New York and by 1700 nearly 2 million acres of land was owned by only five New York families
   4. The English briefly held an alliance with the Five Nations, known as the Covenant Chain, but by the end of the century the Five Nations adopted a policy of neutrality

5. Demanding "liberties," the English of New York got an elected assembly, which drafted its Charter of Liberties and Privileges in 1683

C. The Founding of Carolina
1. Carolina was established as a barrier to Spanish expansion north of Florida
2. Carolina was an offshoot of Barbados and, as such, a slave colony from the start
3. The Fundamental Constitution of Carolina established a feudal society, but did allow for religious toleration and an elected assembly

D. The Holy Experiment
1. Pennsylvania was the last seventeenth-century colony to be established and was given to proprietor William Penn
2. A Quaker, Penn envisioned a colony of peaceful harmony between colonists and Indians and a haven for spiritual freedom

E. Quaker Liberty
1. Quakers believed that liberty was a universal entitlement
   a. Liberty extended to women, blacks, and Indians
2. Religious freedom was a fundamental principle
   a. Quakers upheld a strict moral code
3. Pennsylvania prospered under Penn's policies

IV. Colonies in Crisis

A. Bacon's Rebellion
1. Virginia's government ran a corrupt regime
   a. Good, free land was scarce for freed servants
   b. Taxes on tobacco rose as price fell
2. Frontier settlers demanded:
   a. that the governor remove the colony's Indians to open up land
   b. reduction of taxes
   c. end of rule by the elite
3. Bacon spoke of traditional English liberties
4. Aftermath left Virginia's planter-elite to consolidate their power and improve their image

B. King Philip's War
1. In 1675 King Philip and his forces attacked nearly forty-five New England towns
2. The settlers counterattacked in 1676, breaking the Indians' power once and for all

C. The Glorious Revolution
1. The Glorious Revolution in 1688 established Parliamentary supremacy and secured the Protestant succession to the throne
2. Rather than risk a Catholic succession through James II, the Dutch Protestant William of Orange was asked to assume the throne

3. The overthrow of James II entrenched the notion that liberty was the birthright of all Englishmen
   a. Parliament issued a Bill of Rights in 1689

D. The Glorious Revolution in America
1. In 1675, England established the Lords of Trade to oversee colonial affairs but the colonies were not interested in obeying London
2. To create wealth, James II created a super-colony, the Dominion of New England, between 1686 and 1685
   a. The new colony threatened liberties
3. News of the Glorious Revolution resulted in a reestablishment of former colonial governments
   a. Lord Baltimore was overthrown in Maryland
   b. Jacob Leisler took control of New York
4. In New England, Plymouth was absorbed into Massachusetts, transforming the political structure of the colony
   a. Land ownership, not church membership, was required to vote
   b. Governor appointed in London rather than elected
   c. Colony had to abide by the Toleration Act

E. Witchcraft in New England
1. Witchcraft was widely believed in and punishable by execution
2. Most accused were women

F. The Salem Witch Trials
1. In 1691 several girls named Tituba as a witch
2. Accusation snowballed until, in the end, fourteen women and five men were hanged
3. Increase Mather published "Cases of Conscience"

V. The Eighteenth Century: A Growing Society

A. A Diverse Population
1. As England's economy improved, large-scale migration was draining labor from the mother country
   a. Efforts began to stop emigration
2. Convicts were sent to North America
3. 145,000 Scots and Scots-Irish immigrants came to North America

B. The German Migration
1. Germans, 110,000 in all, formed the largest group of newcomers from the European continent
2. Their migration greatly enhanced the ethnic and religious diversity of Britain's colonies

C. Religious Diversity
1. Eighteenth-century British America was very diverse, host to many religions

2. Other liberties also attracted settlers
   a. availability of land
   b. lack of a military draft
   c. absence of restraints on economic opportunity

D. Settlers and Indians
   1. Indian communities were well integrated into the British imperial system
   2. Traders, British officials, and farmers all viewed Indians differently
   3. The Walking Purchase of 1737 brought fraud to Pennsylvania Indians

E. Colonial Society
   1. The backcountry was the most rapidly growing region in North America
   2. Farmers in the older portions of the Middle Colonies enjoyed a standard of living unimaginable in Europe
      a. Pennsylvania was "the best poor man's country"

F. The Consumer Revolution
   1. Great Britain eclipsed the Dutch in the eighteenth century as a leader in trade
   2. Eighteenth-century colonial society enjoyed a multitude of consumer goods

G. Colonial Cities
   1. Although relatively small and few in number, port cities like Philadelphia were important
   2. The city was home to a large population of artisans
      a. Myer Myers

H. An Empire of Commerce
   1. Trade unified the British Empire

VI. Social Classes in the Colonies
   A. The Colonial Elite
      1. Expanding trade created the emergence of a powerful merchant upper class
      2. In the Chesapeake and Lower South, planters accumulated enormous wealth
      3. America had no titled aristocracy or established social ranks
      4. By 1770 nearly all upper-class Virginians had inherited their wealth
   B. Anglicization
      1. Colonial elites began to think of themselves as more and more English
      2. Desperate to follow an aristocratic lifestyle, many planters fell into debt
      3. The richest group of mainland colonists were South Carolina planters
      4. The tie that held the elite together was the belief that freedom from labor was the mark of the gentleman

C. Poverty in the Colonies
   1. Although poverty was not as widespread compared to England, many colonists had to work as tenants or wage labors because access to land diminished
   2. Taking the colonies as a whole, half of the wealth at mid-century was concentrated in the hands of the richest 10 percent of the population
   3. The better-off in society tended to view the poor as lazy and responsible for their own plight
      a. Communities had policies to warn out undesirables

D. The Middle Ranks
   1. Many in the nonplantation South owned some land
   2. By the eighteenth century, colonial farm families viewed land ownership almost as a right, the social precondition of freedom

E. Women and the Household Economy
   1. Family was the center of economic life and all members contributed to the family's livelihood
   2. The work of farmers' wives and daughters often spelled the difference between a family's self-sufficiency and poverty

F. North America at mid-century
   1. Colonies were diverse with economic prosperity and many liberties compared to Europe

SUGGESTED DISCUSSION QUESTIONS

- Dutch and French society in North America differed in many ways from the English. Discuss some of those differences, including slaves, attitudes toward Indians, trade, settlement, and notions of freedom. Think back to previous chapters as well.
- Eric Foner wrote that "the freedoms Pennsylvania offered to European immigrants contributed to the deterioration of freedom for others." What examples can you cite that prove that statement?
- What reasons were there for the creation of the Dominion of New England? How did the colonists and those in power in England react? Why did the Dominion fail?
- What commonalities were there between Bacon's Rebellion and King Philip's War? How did the two reveal strains in colonial society? How did the colonists in each case use the language of liberty?
- Describe colonial society at mid-century. Be sure to compare the colonial elite to the middle ranks and the poor. What role was there for women?
- How did the colonists benefit from being part of the British Empire?

SUPPLEMENTAL WEB AND VISUAL RESOURCES

The Glorious Revolution of 1688
www.thegloriousrevolution.com/default.asp
This site has a useful chronology, bibliography, and links.

The Middle Colonies
www.kidinfo.com/American_History/Colonization_Mid_Colonies.html
This teacher/parent resource site consists of various links to information on the Middle Colonies.

A Midwife's Tale
www.pbs.org/wgbh/amex/mwt/filmmore/index.html
A Midwife's Tale, a PBS "American Experience" film, recreates the life of Martha Ballard, a midwife from colonial New England. The documentary is based upon the Pulitzer Prize–winning book by Laurel Thatcher Ulrich.

The Pueblo Revolt of 1680
www.pbs.org/weta/thewest/resources/archives/one/pueblo.html
This PBS site offers useful information about the Pueblo Revolt. Also linked is information on the PBS documentary *The West*, the first volume of which covers the Pueblo Revolt.

Salem Witch Trials
etext.lib.virginia.edu/salem/witchcraft
This University of Virginia site is host to the Salem Witch Trials Documentary Archive and Transcription Project.

SUPPLEMENTAL PRINT RESOURCES

Breen, T. H. "'Baubles of Britain:' The American and Consumer Revolutions of the Eighteenth Century." *Diversity and Unity in Early North America,* Philip Morgan, ed. New York: Routledge, 1993: 227–56.

Brewer, John. *The Sinews of Power: War, Money and the English State, 1688–1783.* Cambridge: Harvard University Press, 1988.

Greene, Jack. *Pursuits of Happiness: The Social Development of Early Modern British Colonies and the Formation of American Culture.* Chapel Hill: University of North Carolina Press, 1988.

Harley, David. "Explaining Salem: Calvinist Psychology and the Diagnosis of Possession." *American Historical Review* 101, no. 2 (1996): 307–330.

Nash, Gary. "Urban Wealth and Poverty in Pre-Revolutionary America." *Colonial America: Essays in Politics and Social Development,* Stanley Katz and John Murrin, eds., New York: McGraw Hill, 1983: 447–483.

Ulrich, Laurel Thatcher. *Good Wives: Image and Reality in the Lives of Women in Northern New England, 1650–1750.* New York: Vintage, 1980.

TEST BANK

Matching

e	1. Pope	a. established a Committee of Safety in New York
h	2. Henry Hudson	b. a Protestant who became King of England
i	3. William Penn	c. Metacom
b	4. William of Orange	d. a patroon who owned 700,000 acres in New York
j	5. Samuel de Champlain	e. Pueblo Revolt of 1680
g	6. Duke of York	f. governor of Virginia during Bacon's Rebellion
a	7. Jacob Leisler	g. a Catholic who became King of England
d	8. Kiliaen van Rensselaer	h. claimed New York for the Dutch
c	9. King Philip	i. proprietor of Pennsylvania
f	10. William Berkeley	j. founded Quebec

g	1. Jesuits	a. elites in America becoming more English
c	2. mercantilism	b. allowed Protestant dissenters to worship freely
e	3. Royal African Company	c. government regulations of the nation's economy
a	4. Anglicization	d. Dutch landowners of large estates
h	5. metis	e. had a monopoly on the slave trade
b	6. Toleration Act	f. a very liberal frame for government
d	7. patroons	g. a missionary religious order
j	8. Navigation Act	h. children of French men and Indian women
f	9. West Jersey Concessions	i. believed in the equality of all persons
i	10. Quakers	j. regulated the shipping and selling of colonial products

Multiple Choice

1. Which statement about the Pueblo Revolt is false?
   a. It resulted in a wholesale expulsion of the Spanish settlers
   b. It arose in part from missionaries burning Indian religious artifacts
   c. It resulted in a total renunciation of Catholicism by the Indians

   d. It was successful because the Pueblo peoples cooperated with each other
  *e. It was inspired by Pope, but he died before the actual revolt took place

2. Which European country came to North America for trade and prided itself on its devotion to liberty?
   a. France
  *b. the Netherlands
   c. Britain
   d. Spain
   e. Portugal

3. Which statement about New Netherland is false?
   a. Some slaves possessed "half-freedom"
   b. No elected assembly was established
   c. The Dutch enjoyed good commercial and diplomatic relations with the Five Iroquois Nations
  *d. Women had many liberties, but could not retain their legal identity after marriage
   e. Religious toleration was extended to Catholics and Jews

4. Compared to the other colonies, New York grew relatively slowly because of
  *a. a strong Iroquois control of interior lands and the continued existence of huge landed estates in the Hudson Valley
   b. the decline of the tobacco economy in the colony
   c. the lack of any major city to serve as a magnet to the area
   d. the fact that the Dutch, who controlled the area until 1776, did not encourage immigration
   e. the fact that liberties and freedoms were severely restricted in the colony

5. New France was characterized by
   a. severe conflict between French settlers and the Indians
   b. a well-defined line between Indian and French society
  *c. enduring alliances with the Indians
   d. a Protestant missionary zeal to convert the Indians
   e. its lack of devastating epidemics

6. Which was not a feature of mercantilism?
   a. government-favored monopolies
   b. the favorable flow of gold and silver into a country
   c. countries in fierce competition with each other
  *d. a system of laissez-faire
   e. the promotion of national power

7. Who formed an alliance with the Indians called the Covenant Chain?
   a. Henry Hudson
  *b. Sir Edmund Andros

   c. Duke of York
   d. Kiliaen van Rensselaer
   e. William Kieft

8. The Charter of Liberties and Privileges drafted in 1683 by the New York Assembly
   a. required elections to be held every five years
   *b. upheld the right to a trial by jury
   c. recognized religious toleration for all Protestants, Catholics, and Jews
   d. all of the above
   e. none of the above

9. Carolina grew slowly until
   *a. rice as a staple crop was discovered to be extremely profitable
   b. slaves were brought into the colony
   c. an alliance with the Indians was signed
   d. cotton was introduced into the colony
   e. the king forced the English poor to settle the area

10. To Quakers, liberty
   a. was limited to white, landowning men
   b. was strictly defined
   *c. was a universal entitlement
   d. was extended to women, but not blacks
   e. was limited to the spiritually inclined

11. What was William Penn's most fundamental principle?
   a. political freedom
   *b. religious freedom
   c. equal distribution of land
   d. personal freedom
   e. abolition of slavery

12. Bacon's Rebellion was a response to what?
   *a. worsening economic conditions in Virginia
   b. increased slavery in the Carolinas
   c. Indian attacks in New England
   d. the Glorious Revolution in England
   e. the Salem Witch Trials

13. The Dominion of New England was
   a. a northeastern trade area created by the Navigation Acts
   b. a proprietary colony granted to Edmund Randolph
   c. a system of colonial governance decreed by William of Orange after the Glorious Revolution
   *d. a new unit of colonial administration created by King James II in order to centralize colonial governance

e. a confederation of New England Indian tribes that fought in King Philip's War

14. The Glorious Revolution
    a. ended in terrible bloodshed
    b. resulted in giving the Crown sole power in England
    c. assured the Catholic succession to the throne
    d. had no effect on the American colonies
    *e. placed a Dutchman on the English throne

15. The Glorious Revolution witnessed uprisings in colonial America, including these two colonies
    a. New Hampshire and Pennsylvania
    *b. New York and Maryland
    c. Virginia and New York
    d. Pennsylvania and Maryland
    e. New York and New Hampshire

16. All of the following were factors enticing migration to the British colonies except
    a. availability of land
    b. lack of a military draft
    c. absence of restraints on economic opportunity
    d. religious toleration
    *e. cheap and safe trans-Atlantic transportation

17. The Scotch-Irish immigrants to the colonies
    a. were almost uniformly Catholics
    b. usually worked in the West Indies before moving to the mainland colonies
    *c. were often physicians, merchants, and teachers
    d. did little to add to the religious diversity in America
    e. represented only a small fraction of the immigration to the colonies

18. Indians in eighteenth-century British America
    *a. were well integrated into the British imperial system
    b. benefited from the Walking Purchase of 1737
    c. were viewed the same by traders, British officials, and farmers
    d. never warred with the colonists
    e. had access to the liberties guaranteed to Englishmen

19. What unified the British Empire?
    a. slavery
    b. religion
    *c. trade
    d. political equality
    e. a hierarchal society

20. Of mainland colonists, which group was the wealthiest?
    a. Philadelphia merchants
    b. Boston political elite
    c. Virginia tobacco farmers
    *d. South Carolina plantation owners
    e. New York merchants

True or False

F 1. In the early seventeenth century, London was Europe's foremost shipping and banking center.

T 2. The "freedoms" included in the Dutch "Freedoms and Exemptions" were akin to those of a medieval lord.

T 3. New Netherland never became an important or sizable colony in the Dutch Empire.

F 4. Migration to New France was mostly by Jesuit women who wished to convert the Indians to Catholicism.

F 5. The French, like the English, had a hearty appetite for Indian lands.

T 6. The French missionaries allowed Christian Indians a high degree of independence and did not seek to suppress all traditional practices.

T 7. By 1700, nearly 2 million acres of land was owned by only five New York families.

F 8. Tobacco was considered to be Carolina's "gold."

F 9. William Penn believed in equality and liberty, but not for Indians or blacks.

F 10. Bacon's Rebellion was caused by a conflict between blacks and whites in Virginia.

T 11. A consequence of Bacon's Rebellion was a consolidation of power among Virginia's elite.

F 12. The Glorious Revolution in England was tragically bloody.

T 13. Following the Glorious Revolution, the Massachusetts colony had to abide by the Toleration Act.

F 14. Most of those accused of witchcraft in Salem were young children.

T 15. German migration greatly enhanced the ethnic and religious diversity of Britain's colonies.

T 16. In the eighteenth century, efforts began to stop emigration from England except that convicts were still sent to bolster the Chesapeake labor force.

F 17. The cities were the most rapidly growing region in North America by the mid-eighteenth century.

T 18. Many perceived Pennsylvania to be the best "poor man's" country.

F 19. Anglicization meant that the colonial elites rejected all things British.

T 20. The work of farmers' wives and daughters often spelled the difference between a family's self-sufficiency and poverty.

Short Answer

Identify and give the historical significance of each of the following terms, events, and people in a paragraph or two.

1. Quakers
2. Duke of York
3. mercantilism
4. Salem Witch Trials
5. King Philip's War
6. New Netherland
7. Pueblo Revolt
8. Glorious Revolution
9. Anglicization
10. Consumer Revolution

Essay Questions

1. Between 1650 and 1750 colonial North America encountered a general crisis. Clearly define the colonial crisis and discuss how, as the chapter title suggests, expansion played a role in creating the crisis. Be sure to include in your discussion the expansion of other empires, besides just the British Empire.

2. The colonial crisis was made up of many smaller local conflicts. A common denominator among these conflicts was that the aggrieved groups seized upon the language of freedom to advance their goals. Analyze how various groups used the language of freedom and how successful their arguments were in achieving their goals. What were the different ways "freedom" was defined?

3. The Dutch prided themselves on their devotion to liberty. Explain what kinds of liberties and freedoms the Dutch recognized that other nations, such as England, did not. How did these notions of freedom affect the development of their North American empire? Be sure to include the Indians and slaves in your discussion.

4. William Penn called his colony a "holy experiment." Chronicle the development of Pennsylvania and emphasize the advantages that the colony offered. What liberties were guaranteed and to whom? Be sure to include in your discussion evidence from the *Voices of Freedom* excerpt.

5. The Glorious Revolution solidified the notion that liberty was a birthright of the Englishman. Explain why the Glorious Revolution achieved this idea and

how it subsequently affected the colonies. Did all of the colonists react to the Glorious Revolution the same way? What differences were there? How was the language of liberty used?

6. "Liberty of conscience," wrote a German newcomer in 1739, was the "chief virtue" of British North America, "and on this score I do not repent my immigration." Explain what he meant by that remark. What did immigrants find attractive about the British colonies? What liberties and freedoms were available to the newcomers?
7. North America at mid-century was home to a remarkable diversity of people and different kinds of social organization. In a thoughtful essay, defend this statement, touching upon each of the colonies, the various groups of people living in those colonies, and the freedoms and liberties extend to them.
8. By the 1750s, North American colonists possessed a dual identity—they were both British in their attempts at Anglicization and also distinctly American. What factors contributed to this dual identity? What reinforced the British identity? What reinforced the American identity? Be sure to discuss political, cultural, social, and economic aspects of society.

CHAPTER 4

Slavery, Freedom, and the Struggle for Empire, to 1763

This chapter concentrates on the early history of slavery, political freedoms, and religious revival. The chapter begins with an account from Olaudah Equiano and moves on to describe how slavery fit into a growing world economy. Slavery in the various colonies is compared and contrasted, as well as various forms of resistance practiced by slaves. The next section, on British freedoms, contrasts the enslavement of a people. Highlighting the fact that Britain saw itself as a beacon of liberty, the chapter explains the rights of Englishmen, the rise of republicanism and liberalism, and the limitations of freedom of speech and the press. Suffrage and the role of the elected assemblies demonstrated the autonomy and power the American gentry felt that they had in colonial America. The religious revival movement of the 1730s through the 1760s known as the Great Awakening is explored, showing that the movement helped to inspire the ordinary citizenry belief that they had a stake in the public sphere and a right to speak out, using the language of liberty. The chapter ends with a look at the weaker Spanish and French empires in North America and the clash of interests among the three empires and the Indians that led to the Seven Years' War. The aftermath of that war further changed Anglo-Indian relations, which is highlighted through Pontiac's Rebellion in *Voices of Freedom.*

CHAPTER OUTLINE

I. Olaudah Equiano

II. Slavery and the Empire
  A. The Triangular Trades
    1. British manufactured goods were sent to Africa and the colonies
    2. Colonial products were sent to Europe
    3. Slaves from Africa were sent to the New World

4. Since trade centered upon slavery in some form, free colonists believed that freedom meant in part the power and right to enslave others

B. The Middle Passage
1. The Middle Passage was the voyage across the Atlantic for slaves
2. Slaves were crammed aboard ships for maximum profit
3. The numbers of slaves increased steadily through natural reproduction

C. Chesapeake Slavery
1. Three distinct slave systems were well entrenched in Britain's mainland colonies
   a. Chesapeake
   b. South Carolina and Georgia
   c. Nonplantation societies of New England and the Middle Colonies
2. Chesapeake slavery was based on tobacco
3. Chesapeake plantations tended to be smaller and daily interactions between masters and slaves were more extensive
4. Slavery transformed Chesapeake society into an elaborate hierarchy of degrees of freedom
   a. large planters
   b. yeomen farmers
   c. indentured servants; tenant farmers
   d. slaves
5. With the consolidation of a slave society, race took on more and more importance as a line of social division
   a. Liberties of free blacks were stripped away

D. Slavery in the Rice Kingdom
1. South Carolina and Georgia slavery rested upon rice
2. Rice and indigo required large-scale cultivation, worked by slaves
3. The economy of scale for rice was such that plantations were large
4. By 1770, the number of South Carolina slaves had reached 100,000, well over half the colony's population
5. Georgia was established by a group of philanthropists led by James Oglethorpe in 1733

E. Slavery in the North
1. Since the economics of New England and the Middle Colonies were based on small farms, slavery was far less important
2. Given that slaves were few and posed little threat to the white majority, laws were less harsh than in the South
3. Slaves did represent a sizable percentage of urban laborers, particularly in New York and Philadelphia

III. Slave Culture and Slave Resistance

A. African-Americans

1. The greatest melting pot in American history was the making of an African-American people
2. Most slaves in the eighteenth century were African by birth

B. African-American Cultures
1. In the Chesapeake, slaves learned English, were part of the Great Awakening, and were exposed to white culture
2. In South Carolina and Georgia, two very different black societies emerged
    a. Rice plantations remained distinctly African
    b. Urban servants assimilated into Euro-American culture

C. Resistance to Slavery
1. A common thread for African-Americans was the desire for freedom
    a. Many slaves ran away to Florida or cities
2. The first eighteenth-century slave uprising occurred in New York City in 1712
3. Stono Rebellion of 1739 in South Carolina

IV. An Empire of Freedom

A. British Patriotism
1. Despite the centrality of slavery to its empire, eighteenth-century Great Britain prided itself on being the world's most advanced and freest nation
2. Britons shared a common law, a common language, a common devotion to Protestantism, and a common enemy in France
3. Britons believed that wealth, religion, and freedom went together

B. The Rights of Englishmen
1. Central to this sense of British identity was the concept of liberty
2. British liberty was simultaneously a collection of specific rights, a national characteristic, and a state of mind
3. Britons believed that no man, even the king, was above the law

C. The Language of Liberty
1. All eighteenth-century Britons "reveled in their worldwide reputation for freedom"
2. It was common for ordinary folk to evoke "liberty" when protesting "in the streets"

D. Republican Liberty
1. Republicanism called for the virtuous elite to give themselves to public service
2. Country Party was critical of the corruption of British politics
    a. *Cato's Letters* were widely read by the American colonists

E. Liberal Freedom
1. The leading philosopher of liberty was John Locke

2. Lockean ideas included individual rights, the consent of the governed, and the right of rebellion against unjust or oppressive government
3. Locke's ideas excluded many from their full benefits in the eighteenth century, but they opened the door for many people to challenge later the limitations on their own freedom
4. Republicanism and liberalism would eventually come to be seen as alternative understanding of freedom

V. The Public Sphere
  A. The Right to Vote
    1. Ownership of property was a common qualifier for voting in the colonies
    2. Suffrage was much more common in the colonies than in Britain
    3. Property qualification for holding office was far higher than for voting
    4. By the mid-eighteenth century the typical officeholder was considerably richer than the norm when the century began
  B. Colonial Government
    1. During the first half of the eighteenth century the colonies were largely left to govern themselves
    2. The colonial elected assemblies exercised great influence over the appointed officials
  C. The Rise of the Assemblies
    1. Elected assemblies became dominant and assertive in colonial politics in the eighteenth century
    2. The most powerful assembly was Pennsylvania followed by Massachusetts, New York, Virginia, and South Carolina
    3. Leaders of the assemblies found in the writing of the English Country Party a theory that made sense of their own experience
  D. Politics in Public
    1. The American gentry was very active in the discussion of politics, particularly through clubs
    2. Widespread literacy and the proliferation of newspapers encouraged the political discourse
  E. Freedom of Expression and Its Limits
    1. Freedom of speech was a relatively new idea
    2. Freedom of the press was generally viewed as dangerous
    3. After 1695, the government could not censor print material and colonial newspapers defended freedom of the press as a central component of liberty
  F. The Trial of Zenger
    1. John Peter Zenger went on trial in 1735 for seditious libel
      a. Found not guilty

        b. The outcome promoted the ideas that the truth should always be permitted and that free expression ought to be allowed
    G. The American Enlightenment
        1. Americans sought to apply to political and social life the scientific method of careful investigation based on research and experiment
        2. Deists and natural laws embodied the spirit of the American enlightenment
            a. Benjamin Franklin
            b. Thomas Jefferson

VI. The Great Awakening
    A. Religious Revivals
        1. The Great Awakening was a series of local events united by a commitment to a more emotional and personal Christianity than that offered by existing churches
        2. The Great Awakening was led by flamboyant preachers like Jonathan Edwards
            a. *Sinners in the Hands of an Angry God*
    B. The Preaching of Whitefield
        1. English minister George Whitefield is credited with sparking the Great Awakening
            a. He believed that God was merciful
        2. The Great Awakening enlarged the boundaries of liberty
    C. The Awakening's Impact
        1. The Great Awakening inspired criticism of many aspects of colonial society
        2. A few preachers explicitly condemned slavery, but most masters managed to reconcile Christianity and slaveholding
        3. The Great Awakening expanded the circulation of printed material in the colonies

VII. Imperial Rivalries
    A. Spain in North America
        1. On paper a vast territorial empire, Spanish North America actually consisted of a few small and isolated urban clusters
        2. Despite establishing religious missions and presidios, the population in Spanish North America remained low
    B. California
        1. Spain ordered the colonization of California in response to a perceived Russian threat
            a. Junipero Serra founded the first mission in San Diego in 1769
        2. California was a mission frontier
    C. The French Empire
        1. The French empire expanded in the early eighteenth century

2. The French tended to view North America as a place of cruel exile for criminals and social outcasts

VIII. Battle for the Continent
- A. The Middle Ground
  1. Indians were constantly being pushed from their homes into a "middle ground" between European empires and Indian sovereignty
  2. The government of Virginia granted an immense land grant in 1749 to the Ohio Company
- B. The Seven Years' War
  1. The war began in 1754 as the British tried to dislodge the French from western Pennsylvania
  2. For two years, the war went against the British
  3. The tide of war turned in 1757 with the coming of British Prime Minister William Pitt
  4. The Peace of Paris in 1763 resulted in the expulsion of France from North America
- C. Pontiac's Rebellion
  1. With the removal of the French, the balance of power diplomacy that had enabled groups like the Iroquois to maintain a significant degree of autonomy was eliminated
  2. In 1763 Indians launched a revolt against British rule
  3. Neolin spoke of a pan-Indian identity
  4. To avoid further Indian conflicts, London issued the Proclamation of 1763
- D. Pennsylvania and the Indians
  1. The war deepened the hostility of western Pennsylvania farmers toward Indians and witnessed numerous indiscriminate assaults on Indian communities
  2. The Paxton Boys demanded that Indians be removed from Pennsylvania
- E. Colonial Identities
  1. Colonists emerged from the Seven Years' War with a heightened sense of collective identity
  2. The war also strengthened colonists' pride in being members of the British empire

SUGGESTED DISCUSSION QUESTIONS

- One early American contemporary stated that there was a widespread "dangerous spirit of liberty" among the New World's slaves. Prove that statement by discussing slave culture and forms of resistance.
- Describe slave life in mid-eighteenth century America. How was slavery a

vital component of the global economy? How was it that the making of an African-American people was the greatest melting pot in American history?
- Discuss republicanism and liberalism. What are the similarities and differences between the two concepts? How are they used to enhance liberty?
- Explain why property was important as a qualifier for voting in British America. How did such a policy exclude able voters? Were liberty and property ownership linked? Why or why not?
- How did the Great Awakening inspire ordinary citizens to assert their right to independent judgment? Did the movement expand freedoms? Why or why not?

SUPPLEMENTAL WEB AND VISUAL RESOURCES

Africans in America
www.pbs.org/wgbh/aia/home.html
Africans in America is a four-part PBS video about America's journey through slavery. Part I: "The Terrible Transformation, 1450–1750."

Acculturation
alumni.cc.gettysburg.edu/~s330558/acculturation.html
An excellent site with links to slave literature, art, music, and information on slave resistance.

The First Great Awakening
www.nhc.rtp.nc.us/tserve/eighteen/ekeyinfo/grawaken.htm
This site is designed for educators and offers a considerable amount of information on the Great Awakening. It includes a student discussion and a historian debate section.

Maryland Loyalism
users.erols.com/candidus/
This extensive site includes various links and focuses on the Loyalist movement in Maryland. It includes sound files, documents, and a list of movies relevant to Loyalism in the American Colonies.

American Enlightenment
www.worldandi.com/specialreport/1993/february/Sa10444.htm
The World and I Web site contains a host of educational material and offers a provocative look into the American Enlightenment with arguments against the claim that it existed at all.

SUPPLEMENTAL PRINT RESOURCES

Aldridge, A. Owen. "Natural Religion and Deism in America before Ethan Allen and Thomas Paine." *William and Mary Quarterly* 54, no. 4 (1997): 835–838.

Anderson, Fred. *A People's Army: Massachusetts Soldiers and Society in the Seven Years' War*. New York: Norton, 1985.

Breen T. H. and Stephen Innes. *"Myne Owne Ground": Race and Freedom on Virginia's Eastern Shore, 1640–1676,* New York: Oxford University Press, 1980.

Marsden, George. *Jonathan Edwards: A Life*. New Haven: Yale University Press, 2003.

Sidbury, James. *Ploughshares into Swords: Race, Rebellion, and Identity in Gabriel's Virginia, 1730–1810,* New York: Cambridge University Press, 1997.

Sobel, Mechal. *The World They Made Together: Black and White Values in Eighteenth-Century Virginia.* Princeton: Princeton University Press, 1987.

TEST BANK

Matching

c	1. Olaudah Equiano	a. German-born printer of a colonial weekly journal
e	2. James Oglethorpe	b. Great Awakening preacher
g	3. Pontiac	c. survived the Middle Passage
j	4. Benjamin Franklin	d. founded the first mission in San Diego
f	5. William Pitt	e. Georgian philanthropist
h	6. Jonathan Edwards	f. British prime minister
d	7. Junipero Serra	g. Ottawa war leader
a	8. John Peter Zenger	h. wrote *Sinners in the Hands of an Angry God*
b	9. George Whitefield	i. English Enlightenment philosopher on government
i	10. John Locke	j. founder of the Junto, a club for mutual improvement

e	1. Middle Passage	a. Jamaican fugitive slaves
c	2. Gullah	b. bearers of the good news
b	3. evangelists	c. distinct slave dialect
a	4. maroons	d. no colonial settlement west of the Appalachians
h	5. deference	e. the ship voyage for slaves from Africa to the New World
d	6. Proclamation of 1763	f. right to provide slaves to Spanish America
f	7. asiento	g. the most important product of the European empires
j	8. republicanism	h. courteous respect

i	9. Deism	i. Enlightenment religion
g	10. sugar	j. virtuous elite giving themselves to public service

Multiple Choice

1. What was one consequence for the colonists as a result of constant warfare with France and its Indian allies in the seventeenth and eighteenth centuries?
   *a. reinforcement of their sense of identification with and dependence on Great Britain
   b. a much larger and centrally organized colonial army
   c. a weakening of liberties and freedoms as France continually made gains in North America
   d. a greater hostility towards the colonists from their neighboring Indian communities
   e. a stronger faith and increased membership in the Anglican Church

2. The most important product of the British, French, and Portuguese empires was
   a. rice
   *b. sugar
   c. cotton
   d. tobacco
   e. rum

3. What did the British acquire from Spain in the Treaty of Utrecht of 1713?
   a. Florida
   b. silver
   *c. the asiento
   d. Bermuda
   e. slaves

4. Chesapeake slavery was based upon
   a. rice
   *b. tobacco
   c. cotton
   d. sugar
   e. indigo

5. After experimenting with a variety of crops, farmers in South Carolina and Georgia had the greatest success cultivating
   *a. rice
   b. tobacco
   c. cotton
   d. sugar
   e. indigo

6. The task system
   a. punished slaves for not fulfilling a set quota
   b. allowed slaves to own a portion of the land they worked
   c. meant that slaves were strictly supervised and had little autonomy
   d. was created in response to the Stono Rebellion
   *e. assigned slaves daily jobs and allowed them more free time

7. Georgia was established by James Oglethorpe, whose causes included the improved conditions for imprisoned debtors and
   a. the abolition of indentured servitude
   b. the abolition of a hereditary system
   c. the abolition of taxes
   *d. the abolition of slavery
   e. the abolition of property requirements for voting

8. Why was slavery less prevalent in the northern colonies?
   a. the North was not as racist as the South
   b. it was difficult to transport slaves to the North
   *c. the small farms of the northern colonies did not necessitate the need for slaves
   d. more reformers lived in the North
   e. the northern colonies used Indian labor instead

9. What statement about slaves in the Chesapeake is false?
   a. Slaves learned English
   b. Slaves were part of the Great Awakening
   c. Slaves were exposed to white culture
   d. Slaves began to experience family-centered slave communities
   *e. Slave communities remained distinctly African

10. What did Britons share?
   a. a common language
   b. a common law
   c. a common enemy in France
   d. a common devotion to Protestantism
   *e. all of the above

11. Republicanism
   a. meant a government headed by a king
   *b. celebrated active participation in public life by a virtuous elite
   c. assumed that every citizen was virtuous and capable of holding public office
   d. was essentially individual and private
   e. none of the above

12. Lockean ideas included
   a. individual rights

b. the consent of the governed
c. a "social contract"
d. the right of rebellion against unjust or oppressive government
*e. all of the above

13. Although suffrage requirements varied from colony to colony, the linchpin of voting laws was
*a. property qualification
b. education qualification
c. gender qualification
d. slave ownership qualification
e. religious qualification

14. The assumption among ordinary people that wealth, education, and social prominence carried with them a right to public office was called
a. liberalism
b. Lockean
c. deism
*d. deference
e. suffrage

15. During the eighteenth century, colonial assemblies
a. lost political power to colonial governors
b. remained purely advisory bodies to the royal governor
*c. became assertive and more dominant
d. concentrated on the patronage system
e. rejected the theories of the English Country Party

16. What accelerated the expansion of the public sphere in the eighteenth century?
a. the establishment of various clubs
b. widespread literacy
c. the proliferation of newspapers and libraries
d. the trial of John Peter Zenger
*e. all of the above

17. Deists shared the ideas of eighteenth-century European Enlightenment thinkers that
a. the universe was unknowable
b. Christ's divinity was beyond question
*c. science and reason could uncover God's laws in the natural order
d. God did not exist
e. none of the above

18. The most famous Great Awakening revivalist minister was
a. John Locke
*b. George Whitefield

c. Cotton Mather
d. John Peter Zenger
e. James Oglethorpe

19. Revivalist preachers frequently
   a. called for the abolition of slavery
   b. praised Deism
   *c. criticized commercial society
   d. sought to avoid emotional styles of preaching
   e. none of the above

20. What was the primary purpose of the British when they issued the Proclamation of 1763?
   a. to end the slave trade
   b. to protect the Indians
   c. to open up more land for settlement
   *d. to bring stability to the colonial frontier
   e. to prohibit Catholicism in the newly acquired territory from France

True or False

T 1. Some contemporaries spoke of British America as a "rising empire" that would eventually eclipse the mother country in population and wealth.

F 2. The slave trade was not a vital part of world commerce.

T 3. About one slave in eight perished before reaching the New World.

F 4. Most of the slaves carried to the New World were destined for mainland North America.

T 5. In the Chesapeake, race took on more and more importance and whites increasingly considered free blacks dangerous and undesirable.

T 6. Africans had experience cultivating rice in Africa and helped the English settlers grow it in the South.

T 7. Initially, the proprietors of Georgia banned the introduction of both liquor and slaves.

F 8. In the early eighteenth century, only one-quarter of the urban elite owned at least one slave.

F 9. Most slaves in eighteenth-century British America had been born in the colonies.

F 10. Britons believed that the king was above the law.

T 11. John Locke believed that slaves could not be considered as any part of civil society.

F 12. A higher percentage of the population enjoyed suffrage in Great Britain than in the American colonies.

T 13. In northern colonies the law did not prohibit blacks from voting, but local custom did.

T 14. The most powerful assembly was Pennsylvania's.

T 15. Governments generally viewed freedom of the press as dangerous.

F 16. Deists concluded that the best form of religious devotion was to worship devoutly in organized churches.

F 17. The Great Awakening restricted the boundaries of liberty.

T 18. Preacher George Whitefield proclaimed that God was merciful.

F 19. The Spanish and French North American empires were densely populated areas.

T 20. Pontiac's Rebellion was an Indian revolt against British rule.

Short Answer

Identify and give the historical significance of each of the following terms, events, and people in a paragraph or two.

1. Seven Years' War
2. republicanism and liberalism
3. newspapers
4. European Enlightenment
5. Triangular Trades
6. Deism
7. the Great Awakening
8. Stono Rebellion
9. Benjamin Franklin
10. Pontiac's Rebellion

Essay Questions

1. Explain what one historian meant by the following: "The growth and prosperity of the emerging society of a free colonial British America . . . were achieved as a result of slave labor."

2. The slave experience was diverse in British America. Describe how slavery evolved in the various regions of British America. What liberties, if any, were extended to slaves from one region to another? What was the impact of the Stono Rebellion?

3. While slavery was expanding in British America, so too was freedom. Compare and contrast the simultaneous expansion of freedom and slavery.

How was the concept of "race" increasingly important? Be sure to include Equiano's experience in your response.

4. Britons believed that "wealth, religion, and freedom went together." Explain why they believed those three things went hand in hand. Do you agree with that statement? What evidence is there that proves the statement's validity?

5. The eighteenth century witnessed a considerable expansion of the "public sphere." Describe the various ways in which the colonists participated in the public sphere. Discuss the various clubs that proliferated. What role did literacy and newspapers play? Be sure to include in your discussion who was participating and who was excluded. How was this expansion an expansion of liberty?

6. In *Cato's Letters,* the authors declare, "Without freedom of thought there can be no such thing as wisdom, and no such thing as public liberty, without freedom of speech." Explain how freedom of thought and speech were not absolute rights in eighteenth-century British America. Use the Trial of Zenger to illustrate the limits of freedom of speech. How does *Cato's Letters* help enlarge the sphere of liberty for the colonists?

7. What were the reasons for the revival movement known as the Great Awakening and its effect upon colonial life? Be sure to discuss how it impacted ordinary citizens and how it had political consequences.

8. The European Enlightenment and Deism had a profound impact on the thinking of American colonists. Thoroughly explain the theories that came out of the above movements and how Americans like Thomas Jefferson and Benjamin Franklin responded. What were the implications of these new ideas on American thought and society? Be sure to discuss how each movement expanded the colonists' definitions of liberty and freedom.

9. Explain how the Seven Years' War had a significant impact upon colonial society. Why did the colonists believe that the war was a triumph of liberty over tyranny? What did the war mean for Anglo-Indian relations? Be sure to include in your response the excerpt from Pontiac in *Voices of Freedom.*

CHAPTER 5 — The American Revolution, 1763–1783

This chapter concentrates on the events leading up to the American Revolution and the war itself. Beginning with the dramatic events against lieutenant governor of Massachusetts, Thomas Hutchinson, by an angry mob in response to the Stamp Act, the chapter explains how a crisis against British rule grew from taxation policies. The chapter explains the consequences of the Seven Years' War and the Crown's need for increased revenue from its colonies. Believing that the Stamp Act was a direct infringement upon their liberty, the colonists reacted with indignation and violence. The ensuing decade was fraught with similar calls for the British "enslavement" of the colonists to cease and the rise of opposition groups such as the "Sons of Liberty." When war broke out in 1775, independence was not a clear goal of the Continental Congress. Thomas Paine's *Common Sense* was crucial in educating the common people about their natural right to freedom and liberties that Britain denied. So central is *Common Sense* to the coming of independence that it is featured as the *Voices of Freedom* excerpt for this chapter. The Declaration of Independence, signed six months after the publication of *Common Sense,* forever changed the meaning of American freedom by proclaiming "unalienable rights,"—rights that no government could ever take away. The chapter concludes by chronicling the major battles and strategies of the war, highlighting the treaty that brought France into the war on the American side.

CHAPTER OUTLINE

I. Thomas Hutchinson

II. The Crisis Begins
   A. Consolidating the Empire
      1. Prior to the Seven Years' War, London had loosely tried to regulate some of the colony's economy

2. After the Seven Years' War, London insisted that the colonists play a subordinate role to the mother country and help pay for the protection the British provided
3. Members of the British Parliament had virtual representation
4. Colonists argued London could not tax them because they were underrepresented in Parliament

B. The Stamp Act Crisis
1. The Stamp Act of 1765 was a direct tax on all sorts of printed materials
2. The Act was wide reaching and offended virtually every free colonist
3. Opposition to the Stamp Act was the first great drama of the Revolutionary era and the first major split between colonists and Great Britain over the meaning of freedom
4. American leaders viewed the empire as an association of equals in which free settlers overseas enjoyed the same rights as Britons at home
5. Stamp Act Congress met in 1765 to endorse Virginia's House of Burgesses' resolutions
    a. Patrick Henry

C. Liberty and Resistance
1. No word was more frequently invoked by critics of the Stamp Act than liberty
    a. Liberty Tree
    b. Liberty Hall
    c. Liberty Pole
2. A Committee of Correspondence was created in Boston and other colonies to exchange ideas about resistance
3. The Sons of Liberty were organized to resist the Stamp Act and enforce a boycott of British goods
4. London repealed the Stamp Act, but issued the Declaratory Act

D. Land and Liberty
1. Settlers also cried "liberty" in regard to land disputes
2. The "Regulators" in the Carolinas used liberty to promote their cause
3. Land disputes were behind the creation of Vermont
    a. Ethan Allen

III. The Road to Revolution

A. The Townshend Crisis
1. The 1767 Townshend Act imposed taxes on imported goods
2. By 1768 colonies were again boycotting British goods
    a. Use of American goods came to be seen as a symbol of American resistance
3. Urban artisans strongly supported the boycott

B. The Boston Massacre
1. The March 1770 conflict between Bostonians and British troops left five Bostonians dead
    a. Crispus Attucks

2. The boycott ended after the Townshend duties were repealed, except for a tax on tea
3. The treatment of John Wilkes and the rumors of Anglican bishops being sent to America convinced many settlers that England was succumbing to the same pattern of political corruption and decline of liberty that afflicted other countries

C. The Tea and Intolerable Acts
1. The Tea Act was intended to bail out the East India Company and help to defray the costs of colonial government
2. On December 16, 1773, colonists threw over 300 chests of tea into the Boston Harbor
3. London's response was swift and harsh with the Intolerable Acts
4. The Quebec Act granted religious toleration for Catholics in Canada

IV. The Coming of Independence

A. The Continental Association
1. To resist the Intolerable Acts, a Continental Congress convened in Philadelphia in 1774
2. The Congress adopted the Continental Association, which called for an almost complete halt to trade with Great Britain and the West Indies
   a. Committees of Safety were established to enforce the boycotts
3. The Committees of Safety enlarged the "political nation"

B. The Sweets of Liberty
1. By 1775 talk of liberty pervaded the colonies
2. As the crisis deepened, Americans increasingly based their claims not simply on the historical rights of Englishmen but on the more abstract language of natural rights and universal freedom
   a. John Locke
   b. Thomas Jefferson

C. The Outbreak of War
1. In April 1775, war broke out at Lexington and Concord
2. The Battle of Bunker Hill was a British victory, but the colonists forced General Howe from Boston by March 1776
3. The Second Continental Congress raised an army and appointed George Washington its commander

D. Independence?
1. That the goal of this war was independence was not clear by the end of 1775
2. Opinions varied in the colonies as to the question of independence

E. Common Sense
1. Thomas Paine penned *Common Sense* in January 1776
   a. Called for a democratic system based on frequent elections and a written constitution

2. Paine tied the economic hopes of the new nation to the idea of commercial freedom
3. Paine dramatically expanded the public sphere where political discussion took place

F. The Declaration of Independence
1. The Declaration of Independence declared that Britain's aim was to establish "absolute tyranny" over the colonies and, as such, Congress declared the United States an independent nation
2. Jefferson's preamble gave the Declaration its enduring impact
3. The Declaration of Independence completed the shift from the rights of Englishmen to the rights of mankind as the object of American independence
   a. The "pursuit of happiness" was unique

G. An Asylum for Mankind
1. The idea of "American exceptionalism" was prevalent in the Revolution

V. Securing Independence

A. The Balance of Power
1. Britain had the advantage of a large, professional army and navy
2. Patriots had the advantage of fighting on their own soil and a passionate desire for freedom
3. British soldiers alienated Americans, while citizen-soldiers displayed great valor

B. The First Years of the War
1. The war went badly for George Washington
2. The Battle of Saratoga in October 1777 gave the patriots a victory and boost to morale
   a. The victory convinced the French to aid the Americans in 1778

C. The War in the South
1. The focus of the war shifted to the South in 1778
2. British commanders were unable to consolidate their hold on the South

D. Victory at Last
1. Washington and French troops surrounded General Cornwallis at Yorktown, where he surrendered in October 1781
2. The Treaty of Paris was signed in September 1783
   a. The American delegation consisted of John Adams, Benjamin Franklin, and John Jay

SUGGESTED DISCUSSION QUESTIONS

- Explain why colonists felt that the Stamp Act violated their liberty.
- How did the Stamp Act inadvertently serve to unite the colonies?
- Describe the process from which the colonists concluded that membership in the British Empire was a threat to their freedom, rather than its foundation.

- What made the language of the Declaration of Independence remarkable?
- How can Jefferson's statement that "all men are created equally" be reconciled with the reality of slavery, social hierarchy, and mistreatment of Indians?
- Might the colonists have worked things out with the British or was rebellion inevitable? What might have the British done, if anything, to appease the colonists to avoid conflict?

SUPPLEMENTAL WEB AND VISUAL RESOURCES

American Revolution

revolution.h-net.msu.edu/

This site was created by H-Net Humanities and Social Sciences from the generous support of the National Endowment for the Humanities to serve as a complement to the official companion site to PBS's *Liberty!* documentary series.

Liberty!

www.pbs.org/ktca/liberty/

Liberty! is a PBS documentary on the American Revolution that features dramatic readings from letters and diaries of the period. The series includes: "The Reluctant Revolutionaries," "The Times That Try Men's Souls," and "Are We to be a Nation?"

From Revolution to Reconstruction

odur.let.rug.nl/~usa/D/index.htm#1751

This site contains documentation that was written during the pre– and post–Revolutionary War periods. Documents include *Resolutions of the Stamp Act Congress* and the *Peace Treaty of Paris.*

The Boston Massacre

www.bostonmassacre.net/

This high-quality Web site offers useful insight into the Boston Massacre event as well as excellent pictures and timelines.

The Founding Fathers

store.aetv.com/html/home/index.jhtml

This four-volume set, *The Founding Fathers,* from A&E illuminates the personalities behind the Constitutional debates. This program uses their own words and writings to depict the men who forged the nation. Volumes 1 through 3 are relevant to the Revolution, while volume 4 deals with the Constitution.

Virtual Tour of Revolutionary War

www.ushistory.org/march/

This site offers a breakdown of each battle of the American Revolution and maps help them come alive.

SUPPLEMENTAL PRINT RESOURCES

Bullion, John. "British Ministers and American Resistance to the Stamp Act, October–December 1765." *William and Mary Quarterly* 49, no. 1 (1992): 89–107.

Clodfelter, Mark. "Between Virtue and Necessity: Nathaniel Greene and the Conduct of Civil Military Relations in the South, 1780–1782." *Military Affairs* 52, no. 4 (1988): 169–175.

Jayne, Allen. *Jefferson's Declaration of Independence: Origins, Philosophy and Theology.* Louisville: University of Kentucky Press, 1998.

Kaye, Harvey. *Thomas Paine: Firebrand of Revolution.* New York: Oxford University Press, 2000.

Kruman, Marc. *Between Authority and Liberty: State Constitution Making in Revolutionary America.* Chapel Hill: University of North Carolina Press, 1997.

Maier, Pauline. *American Scripture: Making the Declaration of Independence.* New York: Knopf, 1997.

Resch, John. *Suffering Soldiers: Revolutionary War Veterans, Moral Sentiment, and Political Culture in the Early Republic.* Amherst: University of Massachusetts Press, 1999.

Wheeler, Richard. *Voices of 1776: The Story of the American Revolution in the Words of Those Who Were There.* New York: Meridian Books, 1991.

TEST BANK

Matching

e	1. Thomas Hutchinson	a. offered freedom to slaves if they fought for the British
f	2. Thomas Paine	b. American traitor in command of West Point
g	3. George Washington	c. declared, "Give me liberty, or give me death!"
d	4. Charles Townshend	d. British chancellor of the Exchequer
j	5. Crispus Attucks	e. Massachusetts lieutenant governor
h	6. Thomas Jefferson	f. wrote *Common Sense*
a	7. Lord Dunmore	g. commander of the Continental Army
i	8. Sir William Howe	h. author of the Declaration of Independence
c	9. Patrick Henry	i. British commander
b	10. Benedict Arnold	j. sailor who died in the Boston Massacre

e	1. Stamp Act	a. first significant American victory
i	2. Sons of Liberty	b. beneficiary of the Tea Act

f	3. *Common Sense*	c. religious tolerance for Catholics
h	4. Committee of Correspondence	d. colonists who were loyal to Britain
c	5. Quebec Act	e. viewed by colonists as a major violation of liberty
g	6. virtual representation	f. pamphlet that argued for American independence
j	7. regulators	g. each member of Parliament represented the entire empire
b	8. East India Company	h. exchanged ideas about resistance
a	9. Saratoga	i. organized by Samuel Adams
d	10. loyalists	j. wealthy South Carolina backcountry residents

Multiple Choice

1. What major event led the British government to actively seek ways to make the colonies bear part of the cost of empire?
   a. the Declaration of Independence
   b. King Philip's War
   *c. the Seven Years' War
   d. the Boston Tea Party
   e. the ascendancy of William Pitt as prime minister

2. Britain wished for the colonies to
   a. stop cheating the Treasury by violating the Navigation Acts
   b. contribute to the cost for British protection
   c. accept virtual representation
   d. help pay down Britain's national debt
   *e. all of the above

3. The Sugar Act alarmed colonists because
   a. it increased the tax on molasses and made rum more expensive to produce
   b. it was designed to tax the colonists against their will
   c. it mandated that violators of the Act be tried in a court with a jury
   d. it reduced taxes on rum
   *e. it threatened the profits of colonial merchants already in economic trouble

4. Virtual representation meant that
   a. the colonies elected representatives to the House of Commons
   b. colonial governors served as the colonies representatives in London
   *c. members of the British parliament represented the entire empire
   d. the king appointed representatives for the colonies

e. colonial assemblies sent two nonvoting members to the House of Commons to speak for the colonies

5. Opposition to what act provoked the first great drama of the Revolutionary era and the first major split between colonists and Great Britain over the meaning of freedom?
   *a. the Stamp Act
   b. the Sugar Act
   c. the Intolerable Acts
   d. the Townshend Act
   e. the Declaratory Act

6. The Declaratory Act
   a. placed a tax on all printed documents
   b. declared that colonists had to house British soldiers in their homes
   c. closed the port of Boston on account of the Boston Tea Party
   *d. rejected Americans' claims that only their elected representatives could levy taxes
   e. proclaimed independence from Great Britain

7. Britain's response to the Boston Tea Party was
   a. the Townshend Acts
   *b. the Intolerable Acts
   c. a declaration of war
   d. the Suffolk Resolves
   e. the Boston Massacre

8. The Townshend Acts did all of the following except
   a. impose new import duties on glass and tea
   b. encourage some colonies to boycott British goods
   *c. reaffirm Boston's decision to abide by the Quartering Act
   d. create a Board of Customs Commissioner to catch smugglers
   e. raise revenue to pay the salaries of American governors and judges

9. The Quebec Act
   *a. granted religious toleration for Catholics in Canada
   b. placed a tax on all imported goods from Canada
   c. restricted English migration west of the Appalachian mountains
   d. called for Canada to rebel alongside the Americans for independence
   e. none of the above

10. The Boston Massacre occurred when British soldiers
   a. killed Indians who were raiding frontier towns
   *b. fired into a mob and killed a number of Boston residents
   c. captured some members of the Sons of Liberty who were involved in the Boston Tea Party

d. fired on local minutemen guarding an arsenal
e. were trying to defend Thomas Hutchinson from an angry mob

11. The "shot heard 'round the world'" that began the Revolutionary War was fired from
   a. Boston
   b. New York City
   *c. Lexington
   d. Williamsburg
   e. Hartford

12. Which statement about Thomas Paine's *Common Sense* is false?
   a. It was written in 1776
   b. It called for a democratic system based on frequent elections and a written constitution
   c. It tied the economic hopes of the new nation to the idea of commercial freedom
   d. It dramatically expanded the public sphere
   *e. It was fairly conservative in its arguments

13. The Declaration of Independence
   a. declared that Britain's aim was to establish "absolute tyranny" over the colonies
   b. completed the shift from the rights of Englishmen to the rights of mankind as the object of American independence
   c. declared the United States an independent nation
   d. uniquely proclaimed the "pursuit of happiness" as an unalienable right
   *e. all of the above

14. All of the following were advantages enjoyed by the British during the American Revolution except
   a. the world's best navy
   b. a professionally trained army
   c. the ability to recruit German soldiers to fight for them
   *d. an intimate knowledge of the terrain
   e. the ability to lure slaves to fight for the British in exchange for their freedom

15. The British
   *a. seriously underestimated the support for independence among the population
   b. treated the civilian women with honor and chivalry
   c. highly respected the American citizen-soldier and calculated for his ability
   d. never plundered colonists' homes
   e. treated the slaves as inferior

16. What convinced the French to aid the Americans in 1778?
    a. Washington's abilities as a commander
    b. the French commitment to the ideals of freedom and democracy
    c. the diplomatic genius of Benjamin Franklin
    *d. the American victory at Saratoga
    e. the British naval blockade against France

17. In the winter of 1776–1777, Washington won important victories that improved American morale. These battles were at
    a. Saratoga and Albany, New York
    b. Morristown and East Orange, New Jersey
    c. Long Island and White Plains, New York
    d. Lexington and Concord, Massachusetts
    *e. Trenton and Princeton, New Jersey

18. During the eight years of war, approximately how many Americans bore arms in the army and militias?
    a. 50,000
    b. 100,000
    c. 150,000
    *d. 200,000
    e. 250,000

19. Cornwallis was defeated at Yorktown because
    *a. he had no land or water escape route
    b. he was overwhelmed by Washington's army
    c. General Clinton had withdrawn from Yorktown, leaving Cornwallis vulnerable
    d. most of his troops were cold, starving, and ready to surrender
    e. King George III ordered an end to the war

20. The Treaty of Paris did not
    a. recognize American independence
    *b. sever the alliance between America and France
    c. give America territory between Canada and Florida east of the Mississippi River
    d. give America the right to fish in Atlantic waters off the Canadian coast
    e. guarantee that Loyalists would not be persecuted

True or False

F 1. Prior to the Seven Years' War, Britain had not tried to regulate the colony's economy.

F 2. Although a few were outraged, generally speaking, the colonists were not offended by the Stamp Act.

T 3. American colonists widely believed that Britain had no authority to tax the colonists since they had no elected representative in Parliament.

T 4. American leaders viewed the membership in the British empire as an association of equals.

T 5. The Sons of Liberty enforced a boycott of British goods.

F 6. Ethan Allen led the Hudson Bay Boys in New York to protect the liberties of small farmers.

T 7. Homespun clothing became a symbol of American resistance during the American boycott on British goods.

F 8. Samuel Adams defended the British soldiers involved in the Boston Massacre in a court of law.

T 9. To resist the Intolerable Acts, a Continental Congress convened in Philadelphia.

F 10. The First Continental Congress raised an army and appointed George Washington as its commander.

F 11. Thomas Paine wrote *Common Sense* as a response to Jefferson's Declaration of Independence.

T 12. The idea of "American exceptionalism" was prevalent in the Revolution.

T 13. British soldiers alienated Americans, while citizen-soldiers displayed great valor.

F 14. The American victory at Trenton convinced the French to join the American cause.

T 15. Washington's army was demoralized by repeated failures early in the war and many soldiers simply went home.

T 16. British commanders were never able to consolidate their hold on the South.

F 17. Benedict Arnold almost succeeded in turning over to the British the important fort of Ticonderoga on Lake Champlain.

T 18. The French played a significant role in the surrender of Cornwallis at Yorktown.

F 19. The Treaty of Paris was negotiated quickly after Cornwallis's surrender.

F 20. Americans did not gain much more than independence from the Treaty of Paris.

Short Answer

Identify and give the historical significance of each of the following terms, events, and people in a paragraph or two.

1. Stamp Act
2. Sons of Liberty
3. *Common Sense*
4. Declaratory Act
5. Treaty of Paris (1783)
6. Continental Association
7. Boston Tea Party
8. virtual representation
9. Battle of Saratoga
10. Declaration of Independence

Essay Questions

1. What problems did Britain face after the Seven Years' War and how did it propose to find solutions? How reasonable were London's solutions and how did the colonists view them as an attack upon their liberty?
2. Thoroughly discuss the debates that occurred over virtual representation. How did the leaders in London and the leaders in America view participation in the empire differently?
3. Describe how liberty and freedom were used in both Thomas Paine's *Common Sense* and in the Declaration of Independence.
4. Revolution is a dynamic process whose consequences no one can anticipate. Explain the initial goals of the colonists in 1775 and the evolution of their ultimate decision to declare independence in 1776. What were the consequences of the Revolution by 1783?
5. Many students commonly believe that the Revolutionary War was a short and relatively painless war. However, for Americans, only the Vietnam War lasted longer than the Revolutionary War. In a thoughtful essay, describe why the war was so lengthy and what the costs involved were for the British and for the Americans.
6. Compare the relative advantages of the American and British militaries. How was George Washington able to secure a victory over the most powerful nation in the world?
7. How did the colonists justify their protests and ultimate rebellion? What sources did they call upon? What philosophies were influential? How was the language of freedom and liberty used?
8. As the impending crisis deepened, Americans increasingly based their claims not simply on the historical rights of Englishmen but on the more abstract

language of natural rights and universal freedom. Thinking back to previous chapters, chronicle this evolution beginning with the English Civil War and the Glorious Revolution and following the importance of the Great Awakening and European Enlightenment. Your essay ought to demonstrate the various definitions of freedom and liberty from the early days of settlement to the Revolution.

CHAPTER 6 The Revolution Within

This chapter concentrates on the political and social changes that took place within the American Revolution, focusing on how the concepts of liberty and freedom developed, as well as who gained and lost freedom as a result of the Revolution. The chapter begins with a look at a remarkable American woman, Abigail Adams. The democratization of freedom via the public sphere is explored, looking at state constitutions and qualifications for voting. Issues involving religious liberty are examined through the numerous denominations that sprung up as well as from discussion about the separation of church and state. The chapter also comments on various economic models that competed in the public discourse, emphasizing Adam Smith's theories put forth in *The Wealth of Nations*. Limitations on freedom are then discussed. Those who remained loyal to the British found some of their liberties stripped away, but mostly they were able to reintegrate into society. Indians lost much of their freedom as a result of the war. Slaves believed that the rhetoric of freedom and liberty cried out by the patriots meant that emancipation was also necessary, and they were amazed when they realized that the Americans did not mean liberty for slaves too. Some slaves issued petitions for freedom to New England courts, and excerpts from two of those petitions are the focus of this chapter's *Voices of Freedom*. The war did result in some emancipation, but not in the complete elimination of slavery. The chapter concludes with a look at women and their role in the war as soldier and as "republican mother" charged with the serious task of raising the next generation of republican leaders.

CHAPTER OUTLINE

I. Abigail Adams

II. Democratizing Freedom
    A. The Dream of Equality

1. The Revolution unleashed public debates and political and social struggles that enlarged the scope of freedom and challenged inherited structures of power within America
   a. Rejected was the principle of hereditary aristocracy
2. Inequality had been fundamental to the colonial social order
   a. The Declaration of Independence's assertion that "all men are created equal" radically altered society

B. Expanding the Political Nation
1. The leaders of the Revolution had not intended this disruption of social order
2. The democratization of freedom was dramatic for free men
3. Artisans, small farmers, laborers, and the militia all emerged as a self-conscious element in politics
4. The prewar elite of Pennsylvania opposed independence
   a. This left a vacuum of political leadership filled by Paine, Rush, Matlack, and Young
5. Pennsylvania's radicals attacked property qualifications for voting

C. The New Constitutions
1. All states wrote a new constitution and agreed that their governments must be republics
2. States disagreed as to how the government should be structured
   a. Pennsylvania's one-house legislature
   b. John Adams's "balanced governments" of two-house legislatures

D. The Right to Vote
1. The property qualification for suffrage was hotly debated
2. The least democratization occurred in the southern states whose highly deferential political traditions enabled the landed gentry to retain their control of political affairs
3. By the 1780s with the exceptions of Virginia, Maryland, and New York, a large majority of the adult white male population could meet voting requirements
4. Freedom and an individual's right to vote had become interchangeable

III. Toward Religious Liberty

A. Separating Church and State
1. The drive to separate church and state brought together Deists with members of evangelical sects
2. The seven state constitutions that began with declarations of rights all declared a commitment to "the free exercise of religion"
3. Many states still had limitations on religious freedom
4. Thomas Jefferson's "Bill for Establishing Religious Freedom" separated church and state
5. James Madison insisted that one reason for the complete separation of church and state was to reinforce the principle that the new nation

offered "asylum to the persecuted and oppressed of every nation and religion"

- B. The Revolution and the Churches
  1. As religious liberty expanded some church authority was undermined
     a. Moravian Brethren
  2. Thanks to religious freedom, the early republic witnessed an amazing proliferation of religious denominations
- C. A Virtuous Citizenry
  1. Despite a separation of church and state, public authority continued to support religious values
  2. Leaders wished to encourage virtue—the ability to sacrifice self-interest for the public good

IV. Defining Economic Freedom

- A. Toward Free Labor
  1. The lack of freedom inherent in apprenticeship and servitude increasingly came to be seen as incompatible with republican citizenship
     a. Ebenezer Fox
  2. By 1800, indentured servitude had all but disappeared from the United States
     a. The distinction between freedom and slavery sharpened
- B. The Soul of a Republic
  1. Equality was the very soul of a republic
  2. To most free Americans "equality" meant equal opportunity, rather than equality of condition
  3. Thomas Jefferson, and others, equated land and economic resources with freedom
- C. The Politics of Inflation
  1. The war produced inflation and some Americans took matters into their own hands
- D. The Debate over Free Trade
  1. Congress urged states to adopt measures to fix wages and prices
  2. Smith's argument that the "invisible hand" of the free market directed economic life more effectively and fairly than governmental intervention offered intellectual justification for those who believed that the economy should be left to regulate itself

V. The Limits of Liberty

- A. Colonial Loyalists
  1. Loyalists remained loyal to the crown
     a. Estimated 20 to 25 percent of Americans were Loyalists
  2. Some Loyalists ethnic minorities feared that local majorities would infringe on their freedom to enjoy cultural autonomy

B. The Loyalists' Plight
   1. The War for Independence was in some respects a civil war among Americans
   2. War brought a deprivation of basic rights to many Americans
      a. Many states required residents to take oaths of allegiance to the new nation
   3. When the war ended, as many as 100,000 Loyalists were banished from the United States or emigrated voluntarily

C. The Indians' Revolution
   1. American independence meant the loss of freedom for the Indians
   2. Indians were divided in allegiance during the War for Independence
   3. The British and Americans were guilty of savagery toward the Indians during the war

D. White Freedom, Indian Freedom
   1. To many patriots, access to Indian land was one of the fruits of American victory
      a. But liberty for whites meant loss of liberty for Indians
   2. The Treaty of Paris marked the culmination of a century in which the balance of power in eastern North America shifted away from the Indians and toward white Americans
   3. "Freedom" had not played a major part in Indians' vocabulary before the Revolution but now freedom meant defending their own independence and retaining possession of their land

VI. Slavery and the Revolution

A. Slavery and Freedom
   1. During the debates over British rule, "slavery" was invoked as a political category
      a. Britain was a "kingdom of slaves" while America was a "country of free men"
   2. James Otis wrote of universal freedom, even for blacks
   3. The irony that America cried for liberty while enslaving Africans was not lost on everyone
      a. Edmund Burke
      b. Dr. Samuel Johnson

B. Obstacles to Abolition
   1. Some patriots argued that slavery for blacks made freedom possible for whites
   2. For government to seize property, including slaves, would be an infringement on liberty

C. The Cause of General Liberty
   1. By defining freedom as a universal entitlement rather than a set of rights specific to a particular place or people, the Revolution

inevitably raised question about the status of slavery in the new nation
   a. Samuel Sewall's *The Selling of Joseph* (1700)
   b. Benjamin Rush's warnings

D. In Quest of Freedom
   1. The language of liberty echoed in slave communities, North and South
   2. "Freedom petitions" were presented by slaves in New England in the early 1770s
   3. Many blacks were surprised that white America did not realize its rhetoric of revolution demanded emancipation
   4. Poet Phillis Wheatley and poems by black slaves often spoke of freedom

E. Fighting for Liberty
   1. George Washington accepted black recruits after Lord Dunmore's proclamation
      a. 5,000 blacks enlisted
      b. Some slaves gained freedom by serving in place of an owner
   2. Siding with the British offered slaves far more opportunities for liberty

F. The First Emancipation
   1. For a brief moment, the revolutionary upheaval appeared to threaten the continued existence of slavery
   2. Between 1777 and 1804 every state north of Maryland took steps toward emancipation
   3. Abolition in the North was a slow process and typically applied only to future children of current slave women

G. Free Black Communities
   1. After the war, free black communities came into existence
   2. Despite the rhetoric of freedom, the war did not end slavery for blacks

VII. Daughters of Liberty

A. Revolutionary Women
   1. Many women fought during the war in various capacities
      a. Deborah Sampson
      b. Molly Pitcher
      c. Ladies' Association
   2. Within American households, women participated in the political discussions unleashed by independence

B. Gender and Politics
   1. The winning of independence did not alter the law of family inherited from Britain
   2. In both law and social reality, women lacked the essential qualification of political participation

3. Many women who entered public debate felt the need to apologize for their forthrightness
4. Most men considered women to be naturally submissive and irrational and therefore unfit for citizenship

C. Republican Motherhood
1. Women played a key role in the new republic by training future citizens
2. The idea of republican motherhood reinforced the trend toward the idea of "companionate" marriage

D. The Arduous Struggle for Liberty
1. The Revolution changed the life of virtually every American
2. America became a beacon of hope to those chafing under Old World tyrannies

SUGGESTED DISCUSSION QUESTIONS

- What did Abigail Adams mean when she wrote to her husband, "remember the ladies"? Did she believe in modern female equality?
- Discuss how the struggle for American liberty emboldened other colonists to demand more liberty for themselves.
- How fully embraced was the concept of religious freedom? What evidence can you cite that indicates the young republic was committed to religious freedom? What evidence is there that there were limitations to religious freedom?
- Discuss the various debates held about liberty and slavery. Describe the irony in the American call for freedom while being a slave society.
- The Revolutionary War was empowering for some women. Discuss the various ways that women were able to express greater freedoms and liberties. How did the idea of "republican motherhood" elevate a woman's position?
- Comment on the title of the chapter: The Revolution Within.

SUPPLEMENTAL WEB AND VISUAL RESOURCES

Separation of Church and State

www.infidels.org/library/historical/thomas_jefferson/virginia_act.html

This site contains the text of the Virginia Act for Establishing Religious Freedom.

Abolition

www.loc.gov/exhibits/african/afam005.html

Numerous antislavery newspaper articles and other publications are available from the Revolutionary Era in this site.

Black Service in Revolutionary War
www.americanrevwar.homestead.com/files/BLACKS.HTM
This site concentrates on African-American participation in the Revolutionary War. Links are lined throughout the Web site for further information.

Women in the Revolutionary War
userpages.aug.com/captbarb/femvets.html
This site contains information on specific women, such as Deborah Samson and Nancy Hart, who made a considerable contribution in the Revolutionary War.

Revolutionary War
www.pbs.org/georgewashington/timeline/revolutionary_war.html
George Washington is emphasized in this PBS Web site on the Revolutionary War. Multimedia options are available as well as letters Washington wrote to family and commanders.

SUPPLEMENTAL PRINT RESOURCES

Andrews, Dee. *The Methodists and Revolutionary America, 1760–1800: The Shaping of an Evangelical Culture.* Princeton: Princeton University Press, 2000.

Kerber, Linda. *Women of the Republic: Intellect and Ideology in Revolutionary America.* Chapel Hill: University of North Carolina Press, 1985.

Kulikoff, Allan. "Revolutionary Violence and the Origins of American Democracy." *The Journal of The Historical Society* 2, no. 2 (2002): 229–260.

Mason, Keith. "Localism, Evangelicalism, and Loyalism: The Sources of Discontent in the Revolutionary Chesapeake." *Journal of Southern History* 56, no. 1 (1990): 23–54.

Nash, Gary. *Race and Revolution.* Madison: Madison House, 1990.

Sobel, Mechal. *Teach Me Dreams: The Search for Self in the Revolutionary Era.* Princeton: Princeton University Press, 2000.

TEST BANK

Matching

i	1. Thomas Jefferson	a. black poet
e	2. Adam Smith	b. Pennsylvanian radical
g	3. Samuel Sewall	c. *Thoughts on Government*
b	4. Benjamin Rush	d. thought equality was the soul of a republic
a	5. Phillis Wheatley	e. *Wealth of Nations*
j	6. Abigail Adams	f. director of congressional fiscal policy
h	7. James Otis	g. *The Selling of Joseph*

c	8. John Adams	h. wrote of universal freedom, even for blacks
d	9. Noah Webster	i. Bill for Establishing Religious Freedom
f	10. Robert Morris	j. "remember the ladies"

c	1. virtue	a. raised funds to assist American soldiers
j	2. freedom petitions	b. working for wages or owning a farm or shop
e	3. Loyalists	c. ability to sacrifice self-interest for the public good
a	4. Ladies' Association	d. "school of political democracy"
h	5. republican motherhood	e. retained their allegiance to the Crown
i	6. suffrage	f. fighting for the American cause
b	7. free labor	g. revolution undermined church authority
f	8. patriots	h. responsible for raising the next generation of leaders
d	9. militia	i. the right to vote
g	10. Moravian Brethren	j. action slaves took for their immediate release

Multiple Choice

1. During the American Revolution, what did the patriots reject?
   a. obedience to the male heads of household
   *b. a society based upon a hereditary aristocracy
   c. the establishment of a republic
   d. the definition of liberty as a universal entitlement
   e. none of the above

2. After the Revolution, American freedom would forever be linked with the idea of equality
   a. before the law
   b. in political rights
   c. of economic opportunity
   d. of condition
   *e. all of the above

3. What was used as a sort of "school of political democracy" for the members of the "lower orders" in the colonies-turned-states?
   a. the Protestant Church
   b. the lower house of the state legislatures
   c. the pubs
   *d. the militia
   e. the first public schools

4. Which two states did not follow John Adams's call for a two-house legislature?
   a. New York and Georgia
   *b. Pennsylvania and Vermont
   c. Massachusetts and Pennsylvania
   d. Georgia and Virginia
   e. Vermont and New York

5. Which statement about Pennsylvania is false?
   a. Its prewar elite opposed independence
   b. The radical leadership that emerged included Thomas Paine and Benjamin Rush
   c. The radical leadership attacked property qualifications for voting
   *d. The state did not write a new constitution that favored republicanism
   e. The new government was a one-house legislature

6. With regards to the right to vote
   a. the property qualification for suffrage was hotly debated
   b. the least democratization occurred in the southern states
   c. by the 1780s, with a few exceptions, a large majority of the adult white male population could meet voting requirements
   d. the concept of freedom had become intricately linked with an individual's right to vote
   *e. all of the above

7. During this era, Catholics
   a. had to endure much discrimination throughout the war
   b. were largely Loyalists to the British crown during the war
   *c. saw a dramatic decrease in the amount of anti-Catholicism within America
   d. did not see a change in their status in America because of the war
   e. were outraged when France agreed to help the patriots in their fight

8. For which three accomplishments did Thomas Jefferson wish to be remembered?
   a. president, the Declaration of Independence, the Constitution
   b. Louisiana Purchase, president, Declaration of Independence
   c. the Constitution, the University of Virginia, president
   d. the Bill for Establishing Religious Freedom, the Declaration of Independence, Louisiana Purchase
   *e. Declaration of Independence, University of Virginia, the Bill for Establishing Religious Freedom

9. What was the very soul of a republic according to Noah Webster?
   *a. equality
   b. diversity

c. democracy
d. freedom
e. industry

10. In order to deal with the economic crisis of the war, Congress urged states to
    a. print their own paper money
    *b. adopt measures to fix wages and prices
    c. establish food banks to distribute food to the needy
    d. raise their taxes
    e. all of the above

11. Approximately how many free Americans remained loyal to the British during the war?
    a. 5 to 10 percent
    b. 15 to 20 percent
    *c. 20 to 25 percent
    d. 30 to 35 percent
    e. 45 to 50 percent

12. Which statement about Loyalists is false?
    a. Confiscated property was not returned to them after the war
    *b. Less than 1,000 Loyalists left America after the war
    c. Hostility toward them after the war proved to be short-lived
    d. Loyalists were quickly reintegrated into American society
    e. Soon after the war, most states repealed their test oaths against the Loyalists

13. What did Lord Dunmore do that horrified many southerners?
    a. encouraged Indians to fight for the British cause
    b. was the co-conspirator for a large-scale slave uprising
    *c. promised freedom to slaves that joined the British cause
    d. confiscated property of Loyalists
    e. burned the tobacco fields of patriots

14. Why didn't the American Revolution put an end to slavery?
    *a. The Lockean principle that the government could not deprive people of property applied to slaves, since they were viewed as property, and so slavery appeared as a "right" that could not be taken away
    b. Since all blacks had been slaves in colonial America, the idea of free blacks was unthinkable
    c. Women like Abigail Adams persuaded the founding fathers that women's civil rights ought to come before blacks' civil rights
    d. Thomas Jefferson had absolutely no intention of including blacks when he wrote, "all men are created equal"
    e. George Washington stated that he would not be president if he had to free his slaves

15. After the Revolution, the northern states dealt with the slavery issue by
    a. passing legislation that tightened existing slave laws
    b. passing laws that enacted immediate abolition
    c. mobilizing a mass abolitionist movement
    d. discussing the possibility of secession
    *e. passing legislation for the gradual end of slavery

16. Which statement about blacks and freedom is false?
    a. The language of liberty echoed in slave communities, North and South
    b. "Freedom petitions" were presented by slaves in New England in the early 1770s
    c. Many blacks were surprised that white America did not realize their rhetoric of revolution demanded emancipation
    *d. After the Revolution, emancipation in the North was swift and all-encompassing
    e. Poet Phillis Wheatley and poems by black slaves often spoke of freedom

17. Who did not speak out against denying blacks liberty in America?
    *a. John Locke
    b. James Otis
    c. Benjamin Rush
    d. Samuel Sewall
    e. Phillis Wheatley

18. During this era, women
    a. fought in the war
    b. raised money for the army
    c. served as spies and informants
    d. contributed homespun goods to the army
    *e. all of the above

19. Which statement about gender and politics is false?
    a. The winning of independence did not alter the law of family inherited from Britain
    b. In both law and social reality, women lacked the essential qualification of political participation
    *c. In appreciation for their invaluable contribution to the war effort, women were allowed universal suffrage
    d. Many women who entered public debate felt the need to apologize for their forthrightness
    e. Most men considered women to be naturally submissive and irrational and therefore unfit for citizenship

20. Republican motherhood encouraged
    *a. greater educational opportunities for women
    b. a radical change in the patriarchal structure of the family

c. women to become public speakers for various social causes
d. widespread resentment among women
e. a significant increase in the numbers of women directly involved in politics

True or False

F 1. Part of the philosophy of the Revolution was embracing the principle of hereditary aristocracy.

T 2. The men who led the Revolution from start to finish were by and large members of the American elite.

F 3. Thomas Jefferson's declaration that "all men are created equal" did not radically alter society.

T 4. The men who served in the Revolution through militias were empowered and demanded certain rights, thereby establishing the tradition that service in the army enabled excluded groups to stake a claim to full citizenship.

T 5. The property qualification for voting was hotly debated.

F 6. All states agreed as to how the government should be structured.

T 7. Freedom and an individual's right to vote had become interchangeable by the war's end.

T 8. The War for Independence weakened the deep tradition of American anti-Catholicism.

T 9. Despite the rhetoric of religious freedom, many states had limitations on religious freedom, such as barring Jews from voting and limiting officeholding to Protestants.

F 10. There were very few religious denominations created after the Revolutionary War.

F 11. In spite of the revolutionary rhetoric of freedom, indentured servitude was still widely practiced in the northern states by 1800.

T 12. Thomas Jefferson once proposed that the government give every adult person 50 acres of land if they did not already own land.

T 13. Adam Smith's argument that the "invisible hand" of the free market directed economic life more effectively and fairly than governmental intervention offered intellectual justification for those who believed that the economy should be left to regulate itself.

F 14. For those Loyalists who remained in the United States after the war, hostility toward them proved to be long and intense.

T 15. "Freedom" had not played a major part in Indians' vocabulary before the Revolution but now freedom meant defending their own independence and retaining possession of their land.

T 16. The irony that America cried for liberty while enslaving Africans was not lost on some British observers like Dr. Samuel Johnson.

F 17. As one of the few southern white elite men that did not own slaves, Thomas Jefferson was able to honestly declare that all men had inalienable rights.

T 18. Siding with the British offered slaves far more opportunities for liberty.

F 19. After the war, abolition of slavery in the North was swift and applied to all slaves.

T 20. Until New Jersey added the word "male" in 1897, some of the state's women cast ballots during elections.

Short Answer

Identify and give the historical significance of each of the following terms, events, and people in a paragraph or two.

1. suffrage
2. virtue
3. religious freedom
4. Ladies' Association
5. freedom petitions
6. church and state
7. republican motherhood
8. freedom and slavery
9. Abigail Adams
10. Indians and freedom

Essay Questions

1. Freedom and an individual's right to vote had become interchangeable. Describe how that transformation evolved and how that idea was reflected in the various state constitutions' voting qualifications.

2. Abigail and John Adams exchanged many lively letters. Describe their different or similar beliefs in a proper social order. How far was too far for John Adams?

3. Thomas Paine wrote that the essence of a republic was not the "particular form" of government, but its object: the "public good." Discuss how the various states both structured their governments and how they viewed that their government intended to provide for the public good.

4. Thomas Jefferson claimed that no nation could expect to be ignorant and free. Explain what he meant by this statement. How did he define virtue and how was this quality important to his vision?
5. Using Noah Webster's statement that equality was the very soul of a republic, describe how equality was defined in the Revolutionary Era. Be sure to discuss the many groups that enjoyed equality in America as well as those groups that did not. If equality was indeed the soul of a republic and everyone did not enjoy equality, comment on what the consequences might be for the republic.
6. How did Loyalists view liberty? How were they treated after the war? Why?
7. No one can deny the irony in America's call for freedom from Britain while still being a slave society. Describe the various arguments made by the Americans and British concerning this irony. How was it that some patriots argued that slavery for blacks made freedom possible for whites? How prophetic were others in their denunciation of slavery?
8. How did slaves react to the language of freedom and liberty? Be sure to include in your answer information from *Voices of Freedom.*
9. How did women react to the language of freedom and liberty?
10. Not everyone supported the independence movement within the colonies. Explain who supported independence and who did not. Be sure to include discussion about socioeconomic standing, race, religion, and gender in your answer. Also consider why the other regions of the British Empire, such as Canada and the Caribbean islands, did not also rebel and seek independence.

CHAPTER 7 | Founding a Nation, 1783–1789

This chapter concentrates on the history of early American government and politics. The chapter begins with a description of some of the colorful celebrations held in cities to honor the ratification of the Constitution. The chapter thoroughly explains the strengths and weaknesses of the first written constitution known as the Articles of Confederation. Recognizing that the Articles did not provide the power for a strong central government that was needed to ensure that the republic survived, states sent delegates to a Constitutional Convention to draw up a new constitution. The chapter covers the debates at the convention, discussing separation of powers, division of powers, the debates over slavery, and the final document. Ratification of the document was not a foregone conclusion. Federalists such as James Madison, Alexander Hamilton, and John Jay worked hard at promoting support for ratification by writing a series of essays called *The Federalist*. The Anti-Federalists, who were concerned that the constitution severely limited liberty since it contained no Bill of Rights, opposed them. The *Voices of Freedom* highlights writings from both the Federalists and the Anti-Federalists. A compromise was made when Madison promised the Anti-Federalists that the first Congress would pass a Bill of Rights. The chapter concludes with a discussion about who was included in "We the People." Indians and blacks were clearly not "the people" and the liberties and freedoms guaranteed in the Constitution were not extended to those groups. As the nation consolidated and enlarged the meaning of freedom, a widening gap emerged between "free whites" and "enslaved blacks."

CHAPTER OUTLINE

I. Ratification Celebrations

II. America under the Articles of Confederation
   A. The Articles of Confederation

1. The first written constitution of the United States
    a. One-house Congress
    b. No president
    c. No judiciary
2. The only powers granted to the national government were those for declaring war, conducting foreign affairs, and making treaties
3. Congress established national control over land to the west of the thirteen states and devised rules for its settlement

B. Congress and the West
1. In the immediate aftermath of independence, Congress took the position that by aiding the British, Indians had forfeited the right to their lands
2. Congress was unsure how to regulate the settlement of western land

C. Settlers and the West
1. Peace brought rapid settlement into frontier areas
2. The Ordinance of 1784 established stages of self-government for the West
3. The Ordinance of 1785 regulated land sales in the region north of the Ohio River
4. Like the British before them, American officials found it difficult to regulate the thirst for new land
5. The Northwest Ordinance of 1787 established policy that admitted the area's population as equal members of the political system

D. The Confederation's Weaknesses
1. The war created an economic crisis that the government, under the Articles of Confederation, could not adequately address
2. With Congress unable to act, the states adopted their own economic policies

E. Shays's Rebellion
1. Facing seizure of their land, debt-ridden farmers closed the courts
    a. Invoked liberty trees and liberty poles
2. Shays's Rebellion demonstrated the need for a more central government to ensure private liberty

F. Nationalists of the 1780s
1. Nation builders like James Madison and Alexander Hamilton called for increased national authority
2. The concerns voiced by critics of the Articles found a sympathetic hearing among men who had developed a national consciousness during the Revolution
3. It was decided that a new constitution was needed to avoid either anarchy or monarchy

III. A New Constitution
   A. The Structure of Government
      1. The most prominent men took part in the Constitutional Convention
         a. wealthy
         b. well educated
      2. The Constitution was to create a legislature, an executive, and a national judiciary
      3. The key to stable, effective republican government was finding a way to balance the competing claims of liberty and power
      4. A final compromise was agreed upon based on the Virginia and New Jersey plans
   B. The Limits of Democracy
      1. The Constitution did not set federal voting qualifications
      2. The new government was based upon a limited democracy, ensuring only prominent men holding office
      3. Neither the president nor federal judges were elected by popular vote
         a. The system was confusing
   C. The Division and Separation of Powers
      1. The Constitution embodies federalism and a system of "checks and balances"
         a. Federalism refers to the relationship between the national government and the states
         b. The "separation of powers" or the system of "checks and balances" refers to the way the Constitution seeds to prevent any branch of the national government from dominating the other two
   D. The Debate over Slavery
      1. Slavery divided the delegates
      2. The words "slave" and "slavery" did not appear in the Constitution but it did provide for slavery
      3. The South Carolinian delegates proved very influential in preserving slavery within the Constitution
      4. Congress prohibited the slave trade in 1808
      5. The fugitive slave clause accorded slave laws "extraterritoriality"
      6. The federal government could not interfere with slavery in the states
         a. Slave states had more power due to the three-fifths clause
   E. The Final Document
      1. Delegates signed the final draft on September 17, 1787
      2. The Constitution created a new framework for American development

IV. The Ratification Debate and the Origin of the Bill of Rights
   A. *The Federalist*
      1. Nine of the thirteen states had to ratify the document
      2. *The Federalist* was published to generate support for ratification
         a. Hamilton argued that government was an expression of freedom, not its enemy

B. "Extend the Sphere"
   1. Madison had a new vision of the relationship between government and society in *Federalist Papers* 10 and 51
   2. Madison argued that the large size of the United States was a source of stability, not weakness
   3. Madison helped to popularize the "liberal" idea that men are generally motivated by self-interest, and that the good of society arises from the clash of these private interests

C. The Anti-Federalists
   1. Anti-Federalists opposed ratification
   2. They argued that the republic had to be small and warned that the Constitution would result in a government of oppression
   3. Liberty was the Anti-Federalists' watchword
      a. Argued for a Bill of Rights
   4. Anti-Federalists did not have as much support as the Federalists did
      a. Madison promised a Bill of Rights
      b. Only Rhode Island and North Carolina voted against ratification

D. The Bill of Rights
   1. Madison initially believed a Bill of Rights was pointless
   2. Madison introduced a Bill of Rights to the first Congress
      a. They defined the "unalienable rights" of the Declaration of Independence
   3. Some amendments reflected English roots, while others were uniquely American
   4. Among the most important rights were freedom of speech and the press, vital building blocks of a democratic public sphere

V. We the People

A. National Identity
   1. The Constitution identifies three populations inhabiting the United States
      a. Indians
      b. "other persons"
      c. "people"
         i. Only "people" were entitled to American freedom
   2. American nationality combined both civic and ethnic definitions

B. Indians in the New Nation
   1. Indian tribes had no representation in the new government
   2. Treaty system was used with Indians and Congress forbade the transfer of Indian land without federal approval
   3. Battle of Fallen Timbers led to the Treaty of Greenville in 1795
   4. Some prominent Americans believed that Indians could assimilate into society
      a. Assimilation meant transforming traditional Indian life

C. Blacks and the Republic
  1. The status of citizenship for free blacks was left to individual states
  2. Crèvecoeur's *Letters from an American Farmer* described America as a melting pot of Europeans
  3. Like Crèvecoeur, many white Americans excluded blacks from their conception of the American people
     a. The Naturalization Act of 1790 was limited to "free white persons"

D. Jefferson, Slavery, and Race
  1. John Locke and others maintained "reason" was essential to having liberty
     a. Blacks were not rational beings
     b. Jefferson's *Notes on the State of Virginia*
  2. Jefferson did not think any group was fixed permanently in a status of inferiority
  3. He did not believe black Americans would stay in America
     a. Freeing the slaves without removing them from the country would endanger the nation's freedom

E. Principles of Freedom
  1. The Revolution widened the divide between free Americans and those who remained in slavery
  2. "We the people" increasingly meant white Americans

SUGGESTED DISCUSSION QUESTIONS

- What were the primary weaknesses and strengths of the Articles of Confederation?
- Why was ratification of the Constitution not a foregone conclusion? What were the basic arguments for and against ratification put forth by Federalists and Anti-Federalists?
- Do you believe that the fears of the Anti-Federalists materialized in America? How did the Federalists deal with the Anti-Federalists' concerns?
- What does "republicanism" mean? Why was America a republic, and not a democracy?
- How did blacks and Indians fit into the Constitution? What liberties were extended or denied them?

SUPPLEMENTAL WEB AND VISUAL RESOURCES

Articles of Confederation

www.yale.edu/lawweb/avalon/artconf.htm#art1

This site is produced by Yale University and contains the Articles of Confederation as well as the discussions and debates surrounding it.

Shays's Rebellion
www.calliope.org/shays/shays2.html
With an abundance of material pertaining to the Shays's Rebellion conflict, this site offers a film resource and a bibliography.

Bill of Rights
www.films.com/Films_Home/Item.cfm/1/8099
Films for the Humanities and Sciences offer a video series covering Amendments 1–10.

The Constitution
www.constitution.org/
The Constitution Society has a useful Web site that covers the concepts behind the Constitution, images, and other resources.

Federalists and Anti-Federalists
www.usconstitution.net/consttop_faf.html
This site lists the conflict between the Federalists and Anti-Federalists during the debates before the Constitution was ratified. It lists the events that occurred in each state.

The Founding Fathers
store.aetv.com/html/home/index.jhtml
"A Healthy Constitution" is the fourth volume of this four-volume set from A&E that illuminates the personalities behind the Constitutional debates. This program uses their own words and writings to depict the men who forged the nation.

SUPPLEMENTAL PRINT RESOURCES

Brandon, Mark. *Free in the World: American Slavery and Constitutional Failure.* Princeton: Princeton University Press, 1998.

McCormick, Richard. "The 'Ordinance' of 1784." *William and Mary Quarterly* 50, no. 1 (1993): 112–122.

Newman, Simon. *Parades and Politics of the Streets: Festive Culture in the Early American Republic.* Philadelphia: University of Pennsylvania Press, 1997.

Rakove, Jack. "Smoking Pistols and the Origins of the Constitution." *Reviews in American History* 22, no. 1 (1994): 39–44.

TEST BANK

Matching

j	1. Alexander Hamilton	a. an Anti-Federalist
e	2. Daniel Shays	b. Treaty of Greenville
f	3. Henry Knox	c. *Notes on the State of Virginia*

i	4. John Adams	d. *Letters From an American Farmer*
d	5. Hector Crèvecoeur	e. led uprising of Massachusetts farmers
g	6. George Washington	f. Secretary of War
c	7. Thomas Jefferson	g. willed his slaves to be freed upon the death of his wife
b	8. Little Turtle	h. "Father of the Constitution"
a	9. Patrick Henry	i. served as a diplomat abroad and was unable to serve at the Constitutional Convention
h	10. James Madison	j. author of the most *Federalist* essays

c	1. Articles of Confederation	a. annuity system
g	2. federalism	b. unicam system
e	3. Virginia Plan	c. first written American constitution
f	4. checks and balances	d. slave compromise
h	5. *Federalist Papers*	e. two houses based on proportional representation
b	6. New Jersey Plan	f. separation of powers
d	7. three-fifths clause	g. division of powers
a	8. Treaty of Greenville	h. essays that generated support for Constitutional ratification
j	9. Naturalization Act 1790	i. amendments
i	10. Bill of Rights	j. citizenship limited to whites only

Multiple Choice

1. Under the Articles of Confederation
   a. the government was divided into two houses
   *b. there was no president
   c. there was a judiciary
   d. the government had the power to tax
   e. none of the above

2. The Northwest Ordinance of 1787
   *a. established policy that admitted the area's population as equal members of the political system
   b. regulated western land sales through a policy that was amicable to the Indians
   c. abolished the Articles of Confederation and called for a second Constitutional Convention
   d. was the first step in Alexander Hamilton's plan for economic growth
   e. ruled the West as a colonial power

3. Alexander Hamilton and James Madison were nation builders. What event greatly strengthened the nationalists' cause?
   a. the Anti-Federalist demand for a Bill of Rights
   b. Fries's Rebellion
   c. the election of George Washington as president
   *d. Shays's Rebellion
   e. the passage of the Northwest Ordinance of 1787

4. Shays's Rebellion was significant because it
   a. demonstrated that land distribution policies were out of date
   b. demonstrated that the economic preponderance of the East was bitterly resented by those in the West
   c. demonstrated that the ex-soldiers of the Continental army were unhappy
   *d. demonstrated that the present government was unable to protect property rights
   e. demonstrated that the Indians were causing a problem in the West

5. The relationship between the national government and the states is called
   a. the separation of powers
   b. the New Jersey plan
   *c. federalism
   d. the Virginia plan
   e. the Constitution

6. The new nation had many advantages. What was not an advantage?
   a. its physical isolation from the Old World
   b. a youthful population that was sure to multiply
   *c. it population was overwhelmingly rural and diverse
   d. a broad distribution of property ownership
   e. relatively high literacy among white citizens

7. The Virginia Plan was largely the work of
   a. Patrick Henry
   b. George Washington
   *c. James Madison
   d. Alexander Hamilton
   e. Benjamin Franklin

8. The Virginia Plan
   a. proposed a one-house legislature
   b. offered a compromise regarding slavery
   c. proposed that the head of state be called "president"
   *d. was based on proportional representation
   e. was embraced by smaller states

9. As designed by the Constitution
   a. the president was elected by popular vote

b. senators were to serve two-year terms
*c. the federal judiciary were appointed, not elected by the people
d. House representatives were to be appointed by state legislatures
e. Supreme Court justices were to serve ten-year terms

10. Which statement about slavery and the Constitution is false?
a. The South Carolinian delegates proved very influential in preserving slavery within the Constitution
b. The Constitution called for the end of the slave trade in 1808
c. The fugitive slave clause accorded slave laws extraterritoriality
d. Slave states had more power due to the three-fifths clause
*e. The federal government could interfere with slavery within the states

11. Alexander Hamilton argued that
a. the government was the enemy of freedom
*b. the government was the expression of freedom
c. the government ought to remain weak
d. the government ought to promote liberty abroad
e. the government ought to be subservient to the states

12. The Constitution allowed Congress to
a. pass tariffs
b. coin money
c. regulate interstate commerce
d. issue patents
*e. all of the above

13. Who wrote the majority of the 85 essays in *The Federalist?*
*a. Alexander Hamilton
b. James Madison
c. Benjamin Franklin
d. John Jay
e. John Adams

14. James Madison argued in the *Federalist Papers* that
a. a republic by necessity should be small
b. a large popular democracy was vital for success
*c. a large territory was a source of stability
d. only one or two religions within a nation was best
e. the diversity of the nation was sure to cause anarchy

15. Anti-Federalists included
a. Patrick Henry and John Adams
b. George Washington and John Hancock
c. Samuel Adams and James Madison
d. Benjamin Franklin and John Jay
*e. Samuel Adams and Patrick Henry

16. The Bill of Rights
    a. partly reflected English roots in common law
    b. defined the "unalienable rights" of the Declaration of Independence
    c. was viewed by James Madison as unnecessary
    d. protected religious freedom
    *e. all of the above

17. What two states voted against ratification of the Constitution?
    a. New York and Virginia
    *b. Rhode Island and North Carolina
    c. New York and Rhode Island
    d. South Carolina and Virginia
    e. Delaware and Rhode Island

18. The Treaty of Greenville
    a. ended the disputes between America and Britain over the forts in the West
    *b. ceded most of Ohio and Indiana to the federal government
    c. allowed Indians to petition for citizenship
    d. forbade American settlement west of the Mississippi
    e. allowed local militia to patrol land the bordered Indian territory

19. Which of the following statements about Indians and the new government is false?
    a. Indian tribes had no representation in the new government
    *b. Indians were not mentioned in the Constitution
    c. Only Congress was authorized to transfer Indian lands
    d. Assimilation for the Indians meant transforming traditional Indian life
    e. The treaty system was used with the Indians

20. The Naturalization Act of 1790
    a. allowed all immigrants to become citizens
    b. allowed only Irish, English, and German immigrants to become citizens
    c. allowed everyone except blacks to become citizens
    *d. allowed only white people to become citizens
    e. allowed only white men to become citizens

True or False

T 1. In the immediate aftermath of independence, Congress took the position that by aiding the British, Indians had forfeited the right to their lands.

F 2. At the time of independence, the nation was largely urban, with most of its population residing in the large seacoast cities.

T 3. Congress nearly passed a clause in the Ordinance of 1784 that would have prohibited slavery throughout the West.

T 4. Shays's Rebellion demonstrated the need for a more central government to ensure private liberty.

F 5. The Constitutional delegates that met in Philadelphia represented all of American society, as they were a mix of laborers, farmers, merchants, and politicians.

T 6. The New Jersey Plan proposed a single house legislature, which gave each state one vote.

F 7. "Separation of Powers" refers to the relationship between the national government and the states.

T 8. Alexander Hamilton had proposed that the president and senators serve life terms.

F 9. The Constitution that was ratified in 1788 was America's first written constitution.

T 10. The original Constitution ratified in 1788 does not use the language *slave* or *slavery*.

T 11. Property ownership as a requirement for voting was largely accepted by the founding fathers.

F 12. The Constitution of 1788 defined who could and could not vote.

F 13. George Washington made a significant statement about slavery when he freed his slaves before taking the presidential office.

F 14. The Constitution is a lengthy, wordy document that outlined the structure of government in great detail.

T 15. Anti-Federalists were concerned that the Constitution severely limited liberty.

F 16. Madison argued that the large size of the United States was a source of weakness, not stability.

T 17. Crèvecoeur's *Letters from an American Farmer* described America as a melting pot of Europeans.

T 18. The Constitution left the status of citizenship for free blacks up to individual states.

F 19. "We the people" increasingly meant a melting pot of all peoples.

F 20. Jefferson believed that slaves were fixed permanently in a status of inferiority.

Short Answer

Identify and give the historical significance of each of the following terms, events, and people in a paragraph or two.

1. Shays's Rebellion
2. Bill of Rights
3. Naturalization Act of 1790
4. Treaty of Greenville
5. James Madison
6. Articles of Confederation
7. Northwest Ordinance of 1787
8. *Federalist Papers*
9. slave compromises
10. Anti-Federalists

Essay Questions

1. Compare the strengths and weaknesses of the Articles of Confederation to the Constitution. Which document did a better job at protecting liberties? Running a government? Explain your answer with specific examples.
2. How did the framers of the Constitution balance the competing claims of local self-government, sectional interests, and national authority?
3. Who became full-fledged members of the American people, entitled to the blessings of liberty? Fully explain what criteria were used and who was excluded from membership.
4. James Madison declared, "Liberty may be endangered by the abuses of liberty as well as the abuses of power." This statement reflected a concern that public liberty might endanger private liberty. In a well-thought out essay, analyze this concern. Why might some Americans take this view? Which liberty was more valued? How did the final Constitution reflect this concern?
5. Explain how the slave clauses within the Constitution embedded slavery more deeply than ever in American life and politics, even though they were compromises. Be sure to explain what the various compromises were.
6. Explain the arguments of the Anti-Federalists. How did they define liberty and what role did government have in protecting that liberty?
7. Explain how the Bill of Rights did much to establish freedom of expression as a cornerstone of the popular understanding of American freedom.
8. Using *Letters From an American Farmer* and *Notes on the State of Virginia,* discuss the reach for American citizenship. What did it take to be free and to have liberties in the new nation? According to Crèvecoeur and Jefferson, would there ever be a time when America might be a melting pot of more than just white Europeans?

CHAPTER 8 | Securing the Republic, 1790–1815

This chapter concentrates on the political history of the new nation as it enlarged its boundaries and solidified its independence. Starting with George Washington's inauguration, the chapter explains how the founding fathers believed that the preservation of liberty and freedom for the republic relied upon the success of the American experiment in self-government. Contrasting views as to how government should look immediately emerged with the formulation of America's first political parties. The Federalists supported Alexander Hamilton's program for economic growth while the Democratic-Republicans supported Thomas Jefferson's vision for an agrarian republic. These political debates enlarged the public sphere and an excerpt from one political society, the Democratic-Republican Society of Pennsylvania, is highlighted in *Voices of Freedom*. The chapter then examines the presidency of John Adams, highlighting the restrictions placed upon liberties through the Alien and Sedition Acts. Further restrictions to freedom are explored when discussing slavery and politics and the attempted slave rebellion led by Gabriel. Thomas Jefferson's expansion of executive power is demonstrated with the Louisiana Purchase, which allowed for both western expansion and economic freedom and the eventual expansion of the Cotton Kingdom and slavery. British infringements upon American rights at sea jeopardized American freedom. The failures of embargoes against Great Britain and France led to economic crisis at home and a cry for war from the War Hawks. James Madison declared war against Great Britain in 1812 and, although the war ended by establishing the status quo, it did solidify American independence and freedom from Britain for good.

CHAPTER OUTLINE

I. George Washington's Inauguration

II. Politics in an Age of Passion

A. Hamilton's Program
   1. As secretary of the Treasury, Alexander Hamilton's long-range goal was to make the United States a major commercial and military power
   2. His program had five parts
      a. create credit-worthiness
      b. create a new national debt
      c. create a Bank of the United States
      d. tax producers of whiskey
      e. impose tariffs and government subsidies

B. The Emergence of Opposition
   1. Opposition to Hamilton's plan was voiced by James Madison and Thomas Jefferson
      a. Hamilton's plan depended on a close relationship with Britain
      b. Opponents believed the future lay westward, not with Britain
   2. At first, opposition to Hamilton's program arose almost entirely from the South
   3. Both Hamilton and his opponents used the Constitution as justification of their cause
   4. The South accepted Hamilton's plan after being promised that the national capital would move to the South

C. The Impact of the French Revolution
   1. The French Revolution became very radical by 1793 and France went to war with Britain
   2. George Washington declared American neutrality
   3. Jay's Treaty abandoned any American alliance with France by positioning the United States close to Britain

D. Political Parties
   1. The Federalist Party supported Washington and Hamilton's economic plan, and closed ties with Britain
      a. Freedom rested on deference to authority
   2. Whiskey Rebellion of 1794 proved to Federalists democracy in the hands of ordinary citizens was dangerous

E. The Republican Party
   1. Republicans were more sympathetic to France and had more faith in democratic self-government
   2. Political language became more and more heated

F. An Expanding Public Sphere
   1. The political debates of the 1790s expanded the public sphere
   2. Newspapers and pamphlets were a primary vehicle for political debate
      a. William Manning's *The Key of Liberty*
   3. Political liberty meant not simply voting in elections but constant involvement in public affairs
      a. Democratic-Republican societies

4. Thomas Paine's *The Rights of Man* inspired Republicans
    a. The rights of women
5. The expansion of the public sphere offered women an opportunity to take part in political discussions, read newspapers, and hear orations
    a. Mary Wollstonecraft's *Vindication of the Rights of Woman*
    b. Judith Sargent Murray
6. A common call was for greater educational opportunities

III. The Adams Presidency
  A. The Election of 1796
    1. Adams won with 71 electoral votes and Jefferson became vice president with 68 electoral votes
    2. His presidency was beset by crises
      a. Quasi-War with France
      b. Fries's Rebellion
  B. The "Reign of Witches"
    1. The Alien and Sedition Acts limited civil liberties
    2. As the main target was the Republican press, Thomas Jefferson charged the Acts as reminiscent of the Salem Witch Trials
    3. The Sedition Act thrust freedom of expression to the center of discussions of American liberty
      a. Virginia and Kentucky resolutions
  C. The "Revolution of 1800"
    1. Jefferson defeated Adams in the 1800 presidential campaign
    2. A constitutional crisis emerged with the election
      a. Twelfth Amendment
      b. Hamilton-Burr duel
    3. Adams's acceptance of defeat established the vital precedent of a peaceful transfer of power from a defeated party to its successor
  D. Slavery and Politics
    1. The First Congress received petitions calling for emancipation
    2. Events during the 1790s underscored how powerfully slavery defined and distorted American freedom
      a. Haitian Revolution
  E. Gabriel's Rebellion
    1. Attempted slave rebellion in Virginia, in 1800
    2. The conspiracy was rooted in the institution of Richmond's black community
    3. Gabriel spoke the language of liberty forged in the American Revolution and reinvigorated during the 1790s
    4. Virginian slave laws became stricter

IV. Jefferson in Power
  1. Jefferson's inaugural address was conciliatory toward his opponents
  2. However, he hoped to dismantle as much of the Federalist system as possible

A. Judicial Review
   1. John Marshall's Supreme Court established the Court's power to review laws of Congress and the states
   2. *Marbury v. Madison*
      a. Judicial review
   3. *Fletcher v. Peck*
B. The Louisiana Purchase
   1. To purchase Louisiana, Jefferson had to abandon his conviction that the federal government was limited to powers specifically mentioned in the Constitution
   2. Jefferson's concern with the territory was over trade though New Orleans
   3. Jefferson justified his overreach of the Constitution by securing economic stability for his virtuous agrarian farmers
C. Lewis and Clark
   1. Lewis and Clark's object was both scientific and commercial
   2. Their journey from 1804 to 1806 brought invaluable information and paved the way for a transcontinental country
D. Incorporating Louisiana
   1. New Orleans
   2. Louisiana's slaves had enjoyed far more freedom under the rule of tyrannical Spain than as part of the liberty-loving United States
E. Foreign Entanglements
   1. European wars directly influenced the livelihood of American farmers, merchants, and artisans
      a. Jefferson hoped to avoid foreign entanglements
   2. Barbary Pirates
F. The Embargo
   1. War between France and Great Britain hurt American trade
      a. Impressment
   2. Embargo Act resulted in a crippled U.S. economy
      a. Replaced with Non-Intercourse Act
G. Madison and Pressure for War
   1. Macon's Bill No. 2 allowed trade to resume
   2. War Hawks called for war against Britain
      a. Wished to annex Canada

V. The "Second War for Independence"
   A. The Indian Response
      1. The period from 1800 to 1812 was an "age of prophecy" among the Indians
      2. Tecumseh and Tenskwatawa tried to revive a pan-Indian movement and unite against the white man
   B. The War of 1812
      1. Madison asked for war for the sake of national pride

2. The government found it difficult to finance the war
3. Americans enjoyed few military successes
    a. Peace came with the Treaty of Ghent in December 1814

C. The War's Aftermath
1. The war confirmed the ability of a republican government to conduct a war without surrendering its institutions
2. The war also strengthened a growing sense of nationalism in Canada
3. A casualty of the war was the Federalist party
    a. Hartford Convention

SUGGESTED DISCUSSION QUESTIONS

- Describe how and why political parties arose.
- Explain why Thomas Jefferson thought Alexander Hamilton's economic system "flowed from principles adverse to liberty, and was calculated to undermine and demolish the republic."
- Who did Gabriel think might support his rebellion and why? How was the language of liberty and freedom invoked by Gabriel?
- Why was Napoleon willing to sell the Louisiana Territory to the United States?
- Describe the ironies of the Jefferson administration—compare Jefferson's personal views toward a central government and his actions as president.
- The War of 1812 is sometimes referred to as the Second War for Independence. Do you agree that that is an appropriate title? Why or why not?

SUPPLEMENTAL WEB AND VISUAL RESOURCES

George Washington

main.wgbh.org/wgbh/shop/products/wg065.html

George Washington: The Man Who Wouldn't Be King is a PBS American Experience presentation. The video examines Washington's Revolutionary War years, his relationship with his slaves and fellow founding fathers, and his unshakable commitment to democracy.

Alexander Hamilton

xroads.virginia.edu/~CAP/ham/hamilton.html

This site is a useful resource for exploring Hamilton's political battles as a constitutional reformer. It also includes his background and his changing image through time.

Thomas Paine

www.infidels.org/library/historical/thomas_paine/index.shtml

This site has a large collection of articles written by Thomas Paine. Included are *Age of Reason* and *Rights of Man*.

John Adams

www.pbs.org/wgbh/amex/presidents/02_j_adams/printable.html

The American Experience has a recourse called "The Presidents" on this site. It contains domestic affairs, foreign relations, and presidential politics for each president.

Lewis and Clark

www.films.com/Films_Home/item.cfm?s=1&bin=30313

This site has the video, *The First American Dream: The Journey of Lewis and Clark,* available for purchase. It is a 2000 BBC video production.

James Madison

www.jmu.edu/madison/

This professional site is dedicated to the study and research of James Madison and his time period.

The War of 1812

www.militaryheritage.com/1812.htm

This is an excellent site concentrating on the battles of the war. It includes articles, video clips, animation, and sound.

SUPPLEMENTAL PRINT RESOURCES

Appleby, Joyce. *Inheriting the Revolution: The First Generation of Americans.* Cambridge: Harvard University Press, 2000.

Balieck, Barry. "When the Ends Justify the Means: Thomas Jefferson and the Louisiana Purchase." *Presidential Studies Quarterly* 22, no. 4 (1992): 679–696.

Bolster, W. Jeffrey. *Black Jacks: African American Seamen in the Age of Sail.* Cambridge: Harvard University Press, 1997.

Cornell, Saul. *The Other Founders: Anti-Federalism and the Dissenting Tradition in America, 1788–1828.* Chapel Hill: University of North Carolina Press, 1999.

Edmunds, R. David. *Tecumseh and the Quest for Indian Leadership.* New York: Harper Collins, 1984.

Gilbert, Felix. *To The Farewell Address: Ideas of Early American Foreign Policy.* Princeton: Princeton University Press, 1961.

Knott, Stephen. *Alexander Hamilton and the Persistence of Myth.* Lawrence: University of Kansas Press, 2002.

McCullough, David. *John Adams.* New York: Simon & Schuster, 2001.

Read, James. *Power Versus Liberty: Madison, Hamilton, Wilson, and Jefferson.* Charlottesville: University of Virginia, 2000.

Skeen, C. Edward. *Citizen Soldiers in the War of 1812.* Louisville: University of Kentucky Press, 1999.

Thomas, Ray. "'Not One Cent for Tribute': The Public Addresses and American Popular Reaction to the XYZ Affair." *Journal of the Early American Republic* 34, no. 3 (1983): 389–412.

Tise, Larry. *The American Counterrevolution: A Retreat From Liberty, 1783–1800.* Mechanicsburg, PA: Stackpole Books, 1999.

Tucker, Robert, and David Hendrickson. *Empire of Liberty: The Statecraft of Thomas Jefferson.* Oxford: Oxford University Press, 1990.

Wallace, Anthony. *Jefferson and the Indians: The Tragic Fate of the First Americans.* Cambridge: Harvard University Press, 1999.

TEST BANK

Matching

d	1. Gabriel	a. accused under the Sedition Act
i	2. Tecumseh	b. Chief Justice of the Supreme Court
b	3. John Marshall	c. Haitian salve revolution
e	4. John Fries	d. organizer of a slave rebellion in America
a	5. Matthew Lyon	e. Pennsylvanian militia leader tried for treason
h	6. Mary Wollstonecraft	f. president of the Pennsylvania Abolition Society
f	7. Benjamin Franklin	g. shot Alexander Hamilton in a duel
c	8. Toussaint L'Overture	h. argued certain rights should extend to women
j	9. Henry Clay	i. pan-Indian movement
g	10. Aaron Burr	j. War Hawk

j	1. strict constructionist	a. judicial review
h	2. Jay's Treaty	b. bought for $15 million
d	3. Fries's Rebellion	c. attacked the Sedition Act as unconstitutional
b	4. Louisiana Territory	d. Pennsylvanian farmer uprising
i	5. War Hawks	e. unofficial conflict with France
a	6. *Marbury v. Madison*	f. forced American sailors into the British navy
c	7. Virginia Resolution	g. restrictions placed upon freedom of the press
f	8. impressments	h. negotiated with Britain
g	9. Sedition Act	i. called for war against Britain
e	10. Quasi-War	j. government could only do exactly what the Constitution stated

Multiple Choice

1. George Washington
   a. was committed to party politics and was viewed as one who sought great power
   *b. provided a much-needed symbol of national unity
   c. refused to run for a second term in office
   d. placed John Adams as his secretary of state
   e. had wished to be called "King" instead of "President"

2. Treasury Secretary Alexander Hamilton's long-range goal was
   *a. to make the United States a major commercial and military power
   b. to succeed George Washington as president
   c. to ensure that the American economy grew as an agrarian economy
   d. to build up the Republican Party's strength and power
   e. to end slavery in America

3. Hamilton's economic program included all of the following elements except
   a. taxing the producers of whiskey
   b. creating a national bank
   c. imposing tariffs and government subsidies
   *d. reducing expenditures on the military
   e. creating credit-worthiness

4. Opponents to Hamilton's economic plan
   a. included George Washington
   b. were mostly northerners
   c. believed future growth was to be found through close ties with Britain
   *d. agreed to a compromise that included placing the national capital in the South
   e. were simply jealous of Hamilton's close relationship with Washington

5. The French Revolution
   a. was very conservative when compared to the American Revolution
   *b. reinforced the Republicans' sympathy toward the French
   c. brought American troops to France to fight for liberty
   d. had very little impact upon American foreign policy
   e. had the support of the American Federalist party

6. Who wrote the *Vindication of the Rights of Woman*?
   a. Judith Sargent Murray
   b. Abigail Adams
   *c. Mary Wollstonecraft
   d. Thomas Paine
   e. Benjamin Rush

7. Judith Sargent Murray argued that women's apparent mental inferiority to men simply reflected the fact that women had been denied
   *a. equal education
   b. the vote
   c. rights to own private property
   d. enough leisure time
   e. the ability to earn a living wage

8. The main target of the Sedition Act was
   a. Thomas Jefferson
   b. Federalists
   *c. Republican presses
   d. illegal immigrants
   e. British sympathizers

9. The Virginia and Kentucky Resolutions were a response to what?
   a. the election of 1800
   b. Hamilton's economic plan
   *c. the Alien and Sedition Acts
   d. Fries's Rebellion
   e. impressments of American sailors

10. The Kentucky Resolution had originally stated that
   *a. states could nullify laws of Congress
   b. militia could be called upon to violently put down rebellion
   c. freedom of the press could be suspended in time of war
   d. access to the Mississippi River was reserved only for American citizens
   e. the United States should go to war in 1812 for conquest of Canada

11. Fries's Rebellion
   a. was an uprising in Massachusetts
   b. was provoked because on heavy taxes on whiskey
   c. was bloody and resulted in many deaths
   d. resulted in the execution of John Fries for treason
   *e. resulted in Anti-Federalist sentiment in the region of the rebellion

12. Gabriel's Rebellion
   a. was an attempted slave rebellion in Virginia
   b. was rooted in the institution of Richmond's black community
   c. spoke the language of liberty forged in the American Revolution and reinvigorated during the 1790s
   d. resulted in stricter Virginian slave laws
   *e. all of the above

13. *Marbury v. Madison* dealt with
   *a. judicial review
   b. slaves' rights

c. national debt
d. the appointment of "midnight judges"
e. Indian treaties

14. Jefferson justified his overreach of the Constitution when he purchased Louisiana by citing that
*a. he secured economic stability for his virtuous agrarian farmers
b. there ought to be a loose interpretation of the Constitution
c. industrial growth was assured by the purchase
d. both political parties supported his decision
e. all of the above

15. Lewis and Clark
a. explored Florida
b. were gone for five years
*c. had goals that were both scientific and commercial
d. never made it to the Pacific Ocean
e. were commissioned by James Madison

16. Henry Clay and John C. Calhoun formed a group informally known as
a. Know-Nothings
b. Young Republicans
c. Whigs
*d. War Hawks
e. Peace Doves

17. Jefferson's Embargo Act
a. was successful in restoring freedom of the seas
b. stopped the policy of impressment
c. severely hurt the economies of France and England
d. provoked war with France
*e. caused economic depression within the United States

18. The treaty that ended the War of 1812
a. gave the United States large tracts of land in the west
b. gave Canada the option of joining the United States
c. was a humiliating treaty for Britain
*d. restored the previous status quo
e. resulted in the United States losing land to Canada

19. Which statement about the War of 1812 is false?
a. President Madison asked for war for the sake of national pride
*b. The American victory at the Battle of New Orleans convinced Britain to surrender
c. Americans enjoyed few military successes
d. Peace came with the Treaty of Ghent in December 1814
e. The government found it difficult to finance the war

20. Why did the United States become a one-party state following the War of 1812?
    a. The Republicans were blamed for the British victory in Washington, D.C., and therefore lost power
    *b. The Hartford Convention fatally damaged the Federalist Party, portraying it as treasonous
    c. Under the Alien and Sedition Acts, Madison was able to silence all opposition
    d. Everyone liked James Monroe
    e. The Federalists joined ranks with the War Hawks, taking control of the Republican Party

True or False

F 1. George Washington wore the finest English clothes at his first inauguration.

F 2. Jay's Treaty abandoned any American alliance with Britain by positioning the United States close to France.

T 3. Most of the public government buildings in Washington, D.C., were built using slave labor.

F 4. The Whiskey Rebellion of 1794 proved to Republicans that democracy in the hands of the elite citizenry was dangerous.

T 5. Newspapers and pamphlets were a primary vehicle for political debate.

T 6. Adams's acceptance of defeat established the vital precedent of a peaceful transfer of power from a defeated party to its successor.

T 7. The Twelfth Amendment required electors to cast separate votes for president and vice president.

T 8. Slave artisans played a prominent role in Gabriel's Rebellion.

F 9. The Revolution of 1800 was quite violent.

F 10. When Thomas Jefferson became president he was not interested in dismantling the policies that the Federalists had established.

T 11. Jefferson's interest in the Louisiana Territory was because he wished for permanent access to the port of New Orleans.

F 12. Acre for acre, the Louisiana Purchase was not a bargain.

F 13. The journey from 1804 to 1806 of Lewis and Clark did not produce much valuable information.

F 14. Pocahontas served as Lewis and Clark's interpreter.

F 15. Louisiana's slaves enjoyed far more freedom under the liberty-loving United States than under the rule of tyrannical Spain.

T 16. Tecumseh and Tenskwatawa tried to revive a pan-Indian movement and unite against the white man.

F 17. The Embargo Act was devastating to the British and French.

F 18. The United States military was well prepared for the War of 1812.

F 19. Canadians tried to rebel against Britain during the War of 1812.

T 20. The aftermath of the War of 1812 confirmed the ability of a republican government to conduct a war without surrendering its institutions.

Short Answer

Identify and give the historical significance of each of the following terms, events, and people in a paragraph or two.

1. French Revolution
2. Lewis and Clark
3. War Hawks
4. Whiskey Rebellion
5. John Marshall
6. Alien and Sedition Acts
7. Gabriel's Rebellion
8. Embargo Act
9. War of 1812
10. Alexander Hamilton

Essay Questions

1. To George Washington, "the preservation of the sacred fire of liberty and the destiny of the republican model of government" depended on the success of the American experiment in self-government. What does this statement mean? How and why did Americans come to see that freedom was the special genius of American institutions?

2. Alexander Hamilton's plan called for commercial industrialization. This is something many Americans have viewed positively. Explain why some Americans opposed Hamilton's position. What were some of the alternative plans for development?

3. The men who wrote the Constitution did not envision the active and continuing involvement of ordinary citizens in affairs of state. Describe the various ways ordinary citizens became involved in political concerns. Be sure to include how the concepts of liberty and freedom were used, using *Voices of Freedom*, and explain who was excluded from political discourse.

4. What were the sources of stability and change in the 1790s?

5. The Sedition Act thrust freedom of expression to the center of discussions of American liberty. Defend this statement. Be sure to include in your response a discussion about the Virginia and Kentucky Resolutions.
6. In what ways can Thomas Jefferson's presidency be considered a revolution?
7. What liberties and freedoms were being violated prior to the War of 1812? How did Jefferson and Madison view liberty in terms of British and French behavior on the seas? How did the War Hawks view liberty? Was war the only answer by 1812?
8. Did the United States really win the War of 1812? Examine the terms of the peace settlement. What was gained? What was the larger victory for America?

CHAPTER 9 The Market Revolution

This chapter concentrates on two of the three historical processes unleashed by the Revolution and accelerated after the War of 1812—the spread of market relations and the westward movement of the population. Americans' understandings of freedom were changing to include economic opportunity, physical mobility, and participation in the democratic system. The chapter chronicles the important advancements made in transportation and communication, the growth of western cities, and the expansion of the Cotton Kingdom and slavery. The chapter then explores the market society. Commercial farmers were replacing the self-sufficient farmer. Factory workers, whose labor was divided, replaced the skilled artisan. Labor organizations were established and the workers demanded more rights and liberties. The loss of the artisan is contrasted with the growth of the transcendentalist movement, which called for the triumph of the individual. Likewise, the materialism of the market revolution is contrasted with the religious ferment of the Second Great Awakening. The chapter concludes with a look at the limits of prosperity, noting that women and blacks were excluded from the fruits of the market revolution. As liberty became increasingly identified with economic independence, free blacks were left to the lowest jobs and workingwomen were left with few opportunities. However, *Voices of Freedom* highlights that for one female factory worker, independence was the reason for working in the mills. A cult of domesticity was created by middle-class women and, for them, the ultimate badge of freedom was to be free from work.

CHAPTER OUTLINE

I. The Marquis de Lafayette

II. A New Economy
   A. Roads, Canals, and Railroads

1. Improvements in transportation lowered costs and linked farmers to markets
2. Toll roads did little to help the economy
3. Improved water transportation most dramatically increased the speed and lowered the expense of commerce
   a. steamboat
   b. canals
4. Railroads opened the frontier to settlement and linked markets
5. Telegraph introduced a communication revolution

B. The Rise of the West
1. Improvements in transportation and communication made possible the rise of the West as a powerful, self-conscious region of the new nation
2. People traveled in groups and cooperated with each other to clear land, build houses and barns, and establish communities
3. "Squatters" set up farms on unoccupied land
4. Many Americans settled without regard to national boundaries
   a. Florida

C. The Cotton Kingdom
1. The market revolution and westward expansion heightened the nation's sectional divisions
2. The rise of cotton production came with Eli Whitney's cotton gin
3. The cotton gin revolutionized American slavery

D. The Unfree Westward Movement
1. Historians estimate that around 1 million slaves were shifted from the older slave states to the Deep South between 1800 and 1860
2. Slave trading became a well-organized business
   a. slave coffles
3. Cotton became the empire of liberty's most important export

III. Market Society

A. Commercial Farmers
1. The Northwest became a region with an integrated economy of commercial farms and manufacturing cities
2. Farmers grew crops and raised livestock for sale
3. The East provided a source of credit and a market
4. Between 1840 and 1860, America's output of wheat nearly tripled
   a. steel plow
   b. reaper

B. The Growth of Cities
1. Cities formed part of the western frontier
   a. Cincinnati
   b. Chicago
2. The nature of work shifted from "skilled artisan" to "factory worker"

C. The Factory System
   1. Samuel Slater established America's first factory in 1790
      a. Based on an "outwork" system
   2. The first large-scale American factory was constructed in 1814 at Waltham, Massachusetts
      a. Lowell
   3. "American system of manufactures" relied on the mass production of interchangeable parts that could be rapidly assembled into standardized finished products
   4. The South lagged in factory production

D. The industrial worker
   1. Americans became more aware of "clock time"
   2. Working for an hourly or daily wage seemed to violate the independence Americans considered an essential element of freedom
      a. New England textile mills relied largely on female and child labor
   3. Westward migration and urban development created an energetic, materialistic and mobile population

E. The transformation of law
   1. The corporate form of business organization became central to the new market economy
   2. Many Americans distrusted corporate charters as a form of government-granted special privilege
   3. The Supreme Court ruled on many aspects of corporations and employer/employee rights

IV. The Free Individual

A. The West and Freedom
   1. American freedom had long been linked with the availability of land in the West
      a. Manifest destiny
   2. In national myth and ideology the West would long remain "the last home of the freeborn American"
      a. The West was vital for economic independence, the social condition of freedom

B. The transcendentalists
   1. Ralph Waldo Emerson believed that freedom was an open-ended process of self-realization by which individuals could remake themselves and their own lives

C. Individualism
   1. Americans came to understand that no one person nor government had the right to interfere with the realm of the self
   2. Thoreau worried that the market revolution actually stifled individual judgment

            a. Walden
                i. Genuine freedom lay within
    D. The Second Great Awakening
        1. The Second Great Awakening added a religious underpinning to the celebration of personal self-improvement, self-reliance, and self-determination
        2. The Reverend Charles Grandison Finney became a national celebrity for his preaching in upstate New York
        3. The Second Great Awakening thoroughly democratized American Christianity
            a. Proliferation of ministers
            b. Promoted the doctrine of human free will
        4. Revivalist ministers seized the opportunities offered by the market revolution to spread their message

V. The Limits of Prosperity
    A. Liberty and Prosperity
        1. Official imagery linked the goddess of liberty ever more closely to emblems of material wealth
        2. Opportunities for the "self-made" man abounded
            a. John Jacob Astor
        3. The market revolution produced a new middle class
    B. Race and Opportunity
        1. Free blacks were excluded from the new economic opportunities
        2. Barred from schools and other public facilities, free blacks laboriously constructed their own institutional life
            a. African Methodist Episcopal Church
        3. Free blacks were confined to the lowest ranks of the labor market
        4. Free blacks were not allowed access to public land in the West
    C. The Cult of Domesticity
        1. A new definition of femininity emerged based on values like love, friendship, and mutual obligation
        2. "Virtue" came to be redefined as a personal moral quality associated more and more closely with women
        3. Women were to find freedom in fulfilling their duties within their "sphere"
    D. Women and Work
        1. Only low-paying jobs were available to women
            a. domestic servants, factory workers, and seamstresses
        2. Not working outside the home became a badge of respectability for women
            a. Freedom was freedom from labor
        3. Although middle-class women did not work outside the home, they did much work as wife and mother

E. The Early Labor Movement
   1. Some felt the market revolution reduced their freedom
      a. Economic swings widened the gap between classes
   2. The first Workingmen's parties were established in the 1820s
      a. By 1830s strikes had become commonplace

F. The "Liberty of Living"
   1. Wage workers evoked "liberty" when calling for improvements in the workplace
   2. Some described wage labor as the very essence of slavery
      a. Economic security formed an essential part of American freedom

SUGGESTED DISCUSSION QUESTIONS

- Discuss how Americans' understandings of freedom were changing to include economic opportunity, physical mobility, and participation in the democratic system.
- Discuss transcendentalism and its impact on defining freedom. Who were the major transcendentalists?
- How did America become so productive?
- What were the major aspects of the "market revolution"?
- Explain how the ideology of individualism encouraged political movements.
- Women's experiences in the market revolution were varied. Some women viewed working in the mills as freedom, while others viewed not working as a badge of freedom. Explain this apparent irony.

SUPPLEMENTAL WEB AND VISUAL RESOURCES

Transportation

www.mises.org/journals/scholar/Internal.pdf

This site leads you to a useful essay written by a professor of economics from Loyola College, dealing with the debate of "internal improvements" in the beginning of the nineteenth century.

Cotton

docsouth.unc.edu/chunk11.html

This site from the University of North Carolina documents the cotton industry of the South.

Manifest Destiny

www.pbs.org/kera/usmexicanwar/dialogues/prelude/manifest/manifestdestiny.html

This PBS site offers eight different viewpoints on the concept of "manifest destiny."

A New Nation
www.usembassy.de/usa/history-revolution.htm
This site gives a history of the United States with a specific emphasis on the Revolutionary period and the New Nation. Links and teacher resources are also available.

The Second Great Awakening
www.pbs.org/wgbh/pages/frontline/shows/apocalypse/explanation/puritans.html
This PBS site offers information on the Frontline video *Apocalypse*. There is a list of primary sources and other valuable information pertaining to this topic.

SUPPLEMENTAL PRINT RESOURCES

Field, Peter. *Ralph Waldo Emerson: The Making of a Democratic Intellectual.* Rowman & Littlefield, 2002.

Horton, James Oliver, and Lois Horton. *In Hope of Liberty: Culture, Community, and Protest among Northern Free Blacks, 1700–1860,* New York: Oxford University Press, 1997.

Roediger, David. *The Wages of Whiteness: Race and the Making of The American Working Class.* New York: Verso, 1991.

Sheriff, Carol. *The Artificial River: The Erie Canal and the Paradox of Progress, 1817–1862.* New York: Hill and Wang, 1996.

Whitten, David O. "The Depression of 1837: Incorporating New Ideas into Economic History Instruction: A Survey." *Essays in Business and Economic History* 13 (1995): 27–40.

TEST BANK

Matching

e	1. Robert Fulton	a. Supreme Court chief justice
f	2. Richard Allen	b. transcendentalist
g	3. Josephine Baker	c. coined the term "manifest destiny"
a	4. Roger Taney	d. established America's first factory
c	5. John O'Sullivan	e. steamboat innovator
i	6. Charles G. Finney	f. African Methodist Episcopal Church
h	7. John Jacob Astor	g. Lowell factory worker
j	8. Alexis de Tocqueville	h. self-made millionaire
b	9. Ralph Waldo Emerson	i. preacher in New York
d	10. Samuel Slater	j. *Democracy in America*

f	1. Second Great Awakening	a. a celebration of the home
a	2. cult of domesticity	b. revolutionized American slavery
j	3. corporation	c. mass production of interchangeable parts
h	4. transcendentalism	d. a personal moral quality associated with women
i	5. slave coffles	e. a belief that American expansion was divinely appointed
g	6. *Commonwealth v. Hunt*	f. religious revival
b	7. cotton gin	g. a decree that labor organization was legal
c	8. American system of manufactures	h. a literary and philosophical movement
e	9. manifest destiny	i. groups chained together while migrating to the Deep South
d	10. virtue	j. a charted entity that has rights and liabilities distinct from those of its members

Multiple Choice

1. What improvement most dramatically increased the speed and lowered the expense of commerce?
   a. steel tracks for railroads
   *b. canals and steamboats
   c. better communication via the telegraph
   d. revenue-making roads like "turnpikes"
   e. the establishment of an efficient postal system

2. America's first commercial railroad was
   a. Pennsylvania Railroad
   b. Union-Pacific Railroad
   c. Reading Railroad
   *d. Baltimore & Ohio Railroad
   e. South Carolina Railroad

3. Which statement about the western settlements is false?
   a. Squatters set up farms on unoccupied land
   b. People cooperated with each other to clear land and build shelters
   *c. The government discouraged western settlement at every turn
   d. Americans settled without regard to national boundaries
   e. Improvements in transportation and communication accelerated its settlement

4. What statement about the Erie Canal is false?
   *a. It was completed in 1845

b. At 363 miles, it was the longest man-made canal to date
c. It connected the Great Lakes with New York City
d. Its completion attracted an influx of farmers migrating to that area
e. It was successful in reducing travel time and shipping costs

5. The first industry to be shaped by the large factory system was
*a. textiles
b. guns
c. iron works
d. pottery
e. shoemaking

6. Women workers at the Lowell mills
a. never had time to make friends
b. commuted to work daily from their family farms
c. quickly organized a union to strike for higher wages
d. held management positions
*e. lived in closely supervised boardinghouses

7. What was the most important export for America by the mid-nineteenth century?
a. tobacco
b. coal
c. timber
*d. cotton
e. wheat

8. In 1793, the United States produced 5 million pounds of cotton, compared to the _____ million pounds it produced by 1820.
a. 20
b. 70
c. 120
*d. 170
e. 220

9. John Deere and Cyrus McCormick invented what, respectively?
a. cotton gin and reaper
b. telegraph and steel plow
*c. steel plow and reaper
d. standard railroad gauge and cotton gin
e. steel plow and cotton gin

10. Which statement about corporations is false?
a. A corporation could fail without ruining its directors and stockholders
*b. The corporation was not a vital component in the new market economy
c. A corporation enjoyed special privileges and powers granted in a charter from the government

d. Corporations were able to raise far more capital than the traditional forms of enterprise
e. Many Americans distrusted corporate charters as a form of government-granted special privilege

11. In *Gibbons v. Ogden* the Supreme Court ruled that
   a. the Louisiana Purchase was unconstitutional
   b. Florida was annexed by the United States illegally
   *c. a monopoly on steam navigation between New York and New Jersey granted by the state of New York was unconstitutional
   d. corporations were illegal because their potential to become monopolistic posed a threat to individual free enterprise
   e. railroad workers had no right to strike since it interfered with national commerce

12. The transcendentalist movement
   *a. called for the triumph of the individual
   b. is also known as the "Second Great Awakening"
   c. stressed teamwork in order to industrialize
   d. was largely based in the South
   e. marked the early beginnings of the environmental movement

13. Henry David Thoreau believed that
   a. economic independence was essential for freedom
   *b. genuine freedom lay within
   c. the market revolution brought freedom to many
   d. true freedom was not obtainable
   e. government was the ultimate expression of freedom

14. Which statement about the Second Great Awakening is false?
   a. The Second Great Awakening added a religious underpinning to the celebration of personal self-improvement, self-reliance, and self-determination
   b. The Reverend Charles Grandison Finney became a national celebrity for his preaching in upstate New York
   *c. The Second Great Awakening was concentrated within the Congressional Church
   d. The Second Great Awakening thoroughly democratized American Christianity
   e. Revivalist ministers seized the opportunities offered by the market revolution to spread their message

15. Which denomination enjoyed the largest membership in America by the 1840s?
   *a. Methodist
   b. Congregationalist
   c. Baptist

d. Presbyterian
e. Episcopal

16. During the market revolution, official imagery linked the goddess of liberty ever more closely to
   a. the right to vote
   *b. emblems of material wealth
   c. idols of worship
   d. the freedom of wage-labor
   e. all of the above

17. Which statement about opportunities for blacks in America during the market revolution is false?
   *a. Free blacks prospered greatly from the skilled jobs that opened up to them in the new western cities
   b. Free blacks were excluded from the new economic opportunities
   c. Free blacks were barred from schools and other public facilities and so constructed their own institutional life
   d. Free blacks were confined to the lowest ranks of the labor market
   e. Free blacks were not allowed access to public land in the West

18. What helped to encourage Richard Allen to establish the African Methodist Episcopal Church?
   a. He did not get along with the white minister at his former place of worship
   *b. He was forcibly removed from praying at the altar rail at his former place of worship
   c. He wanted to see an integrated church that combined the elements he enjoyed most from the Methodists and the Episcopalians
   d. Frederick Douglass gave him a generous grant to establish a new church
   e. Great Awakening minister Charles G. Finney persuaded Allen to build a black church since Finney believed worship should be segregated

19. The role of white middle-class women in antebellum America was primarily
   a. to pursue a college education
   b. to take a job outside the home to supplement the family's disposable income
   c. to have as large a family as possible
   *d. to focus her energies on the home and children
   e. to produce the daily foodstuffs and necessities that her household required

20. In his essay "The Laboring Classes," Orestes Brownson believed that
   *a. wealth and labor were at war
   b. workers' problems had to be understood as individual

c. the solution to labor's problems required less government intervention
d. the workers were essentially lazy and corrupted by the temptations of the saloon
e. the market revolution had allowed the laboring classes to achieve true freedom

True or False

T 1. The catalyst for the market revolution was a series of innovations in transportation and communication.

T 2. The market revolution produced a new middle class.

F 3. Toll roads did much to help the economy.

T 4. After 1814, commercial farmers began replacing the self-sufficient farmer, while factory workers began replacing the skilled artisan.

T 5. Because an English law forbade the export of machinery blueprints, Samuel Slater memorized the plans for the power-driven spinning jenny before immigrating to America.

T 6. In order to satisfy the need for slave labor in the Cotton Kingdom, it is estimated that about 1 million slaves were relocated to the Deep South from the older slave states between 1800 and 1860.

T 7. By the 1850s, Massachusetts had become the second most industrialized region of the world, after Great Britain.

T 8. The early industrial revolution in America was largely confined to New England and a few cities outside it.

F 9. During the market revolution, the separation of classes shrunk as economic equality was more evenly distributed, as seen with the declining rate of bankruptcy.

F 10. National boundaries made westward expansion difficult as they erected a barrier to settlement.

T 11. John O'Sullivan coined the term "manifest destiny" to describe America's divinely appointed mission to settle all of North America.

F 12. Henry David Thoreau celebrated the innovation of the market revolution.

T 13. The religious revivals of the early nineteenth century were originally organized by established religious leaders who were alarmed by the low levels of church attendance in the young republic.

F 14. One significant way that blacks were able to enjoy economic independence was by settling in the West on federally provided public land.

F 15. Despite the fact that the first Workingman's Parties had been established by the 1820s, strikes were still very uncommon in the 1830s.

T 16. Under the dictates of the "cult of domesticity," women were to find freedom in fulfilling their duties within their "sphere."

F 17. There was a significant increase in the American birthrate during the nineteenth century.

F 18. Women and blacks were included in the fruits of the market revolution.

T 19. For middle-class women in the nineteenth century, not working was viewed as a badge of freedom.

T 20. As the market revolution took on steam, some critics described wage labor as the very essence of slavery.

Short Answer

Identify and give the historical significance of each of the following terms, events, and people in a paragraph or two.

1. factory system
2. individualism
3. corporations
4. transcendentalism
5. rise of the West
6. Erie Canal
7. Charles G. Finney
8. cult of domesticity
9. free blacks
10. Lowell factories

Essay Questions

1. The Marquis de Lafayette, who fought for American independence and revisited the United States fifty years later, wrote that he "would never have drawn my sword in the cause of America if I could have conceived that thereby I was founding a land of slavery." What might Lafayette have seen in 1824 America that would impel him to make such a statement? How had slavery evolved? Was it expanding? How entrenched in American life was it at this time?
2. Explain how improvements in transportation and communication made possible the rise of the West as a powerful, self-conscious region of the new nation.

3. Two groups of people were left out of the market revolution: women and blacks. Describe their experiences.

4. Explain the shift from artisan to factory worker, and discuss the factory system. What were the advantages and disadvantages? Who was left out? Who benefited? What were some ways workers responded?

5. Thoroughly describe the arguments that linked American freedom to westward expansion. Who or what were obstacles to freedom in the pursuit of expansion? How did Americans deal with those obstacles?

6. Explain how transcendentalism and the Second Great Awakening affected the definitions of freedom. How were both movements a response to the market revolution?

7. Comment on what Alexis de Tocqueville meant when he said that Americans "combine the notions of Christianity and of liberty so intimately in their minds that it is impossible to make them conceive the one without the other." How accurate do you think that observation was?

8. Some women worked in the mills while others developed a "cult of domesticity." Compare the meaning of freedom for both of these groups of women. Be sure to use the *Voices of Freedom* excerpt in your response. Think back to previous chapters and compare the role of women during the market revolution to their "republican motherhood" role during the American Revolution.

9. Describe how the laboring class used the language of slavery and freedom. What were some of the arguments put forth by men like Langdon Byllesby, Ralph Waldo Emerson, and Orestes Brownson?

CHAPTER 10

Democracy in America, 1815–1840

This chapter concentrates on the last of the three historical processes unleashed by the Revolution and accelerated after the War of 1812—the rise of a vigorous political democracy. Democracy triumphed as the electorate enlarged with the abolishment of property requirements for suffrage. *Voices of Freedom* highlights the argument of a non-landholding citizen for suffrage. However, as with the market revolution, women and blacks were excluded from political democracy. The War of 1812 put into motion the market revolution and national leaders understood that the federal government had a responsibility to ensure economic growth for America. "The American System" was a political program for economic growth and the chapter explains the role of banks, transportation, and economic recessions. The 1820 Missouri Compromise is discussed by highlighting sectional divisions in the country. Increased American power in the Western Hemisphere is shown with the Monroe Doctrine and the nationalist agenda of John Quincy Adams. The emergence of political parties is explored, highlighting Martin Van Buren's beliefs that party politics was an important component in ensuring liberty for the American people. The chapter then chronicles the presidency of Andrew Jackson. Guiding the nation through a nullification crisis, the removal of Indians from the southeast, and a bank war, Jackson's commitment to states' rights was challenged. Once again, sectionalism and the power of the South in Congress are seen with the nullification crisis. Jackson, and Whigs such as Daniel Webster, supported Union and liberty; while supporters of nullification cried that the federal government was overstepping its rights and infringing upon states' liberty. Likewise, the South's desire to expand the Cotton Kingdom forced the removal of "civilized" Indians who had adopted many American ways. Finally, the chapter concludes with the bank wars and Jackson's veto to extend the life of the Second Bank of the United States. The Panic of 1837 and subsequent depression allowed the Whig William Henry Harrison to reach the White House in 1840, only to pass away a month after the inauguration.

CHAPTER OUTLINE

I. Andrew Jackson

II. The Triumph of Democracy
  A. Property and Democracy
    1. Property requirements for voting were eliminated by states
  B. The Dorr War
    1. Rhode Island was an exception
    2. Wage earners organized the People's Convention in 1841
      a. Elected Thomas Dorr
  C. Democracy in America
    1. By 1840, more than 90 percent of adult white men were eligible to vote
    2. Democratic political institutions came to define the nation's sense of its own identity
    3. Tocqueville identified democracy as an essential attribute of American freedom
    4. The term "citizen" in America had become synonymous with the right to vote
    5. As with the market revolution, women and blacks were barred from full democracy
      a. They were denied on the basis of natural incapacity
  D. Women and the Public Sphere
    1. Rise of the mass circulation "penny press"
    2. The growth of the reading public opened the door for the rise of a new generation of women writers
  E. A Racial Democracy
    1. Despite increased democracy in America, blacks were seen as a group apart
    2. Blacks were often portrayed as stereotypes
    3. Blacks were not allowed to vote in most states
    4. In effect, race had replaced class as the boundary that separated those American men who were entitled to enjoy political freedom from those who were not

III. Nationalism and Its Discontents
  A. The American System
    1. A new manufacturing sector emerged from the War of 1812 and many believed that it was necessary complement to the agricultural sector for national growth
    2. In 1815 President James Madison put forward a blueprint for government-promoted economic development that came to be known as the American System
      a. new national bank
      b. tariffs
      c. federal financing for better roads and canals

3. President Madison came to believe that a constitutional amendment was necessary for the government to build roads and canals

B. Banks and Money
1. The Second Bank of the United States was a profit-making corporation that served the government
2. Local banks promoted economic growth
3. Local banks printed money
   a. Value of paper currency fluctuated wildly
   b. Bank of the United States was supposed to prevent the over-issuance of money

C. The Panic of 1819
1. The Bank of the United States participated in a speculative fever that swept the country after the War of 1812 ended
2. Early in 1819, as European demand for American farm products returned to normal levels, the economic bubble burst
3. The Panic of 1819 disrupted the political harmony of the previous years
   a. Americans continued to distrust banks
4. The Supreme Court ruled in *McCulloch v. Maryland* that the Bank of the United States was constitutional
   a. Maryland could not tax the bank

D. The Missouri Controversy
1. James Monroe's two terms as president were characterized by the absence of two-party competition
2. The absence of political party disputes was replaced by sectional disputes
3. Missouri petitioned for statehood in 1819
   a. Debate arose over slavery
4. Missouri Compromise was adopted by Congress in 1820
   a. Henry Clay engineered a second Missouri Compromise
5. Northern Republicans did not want slavery to expand for political reasons
6. The Missouri debate highlighted that the westward expansion of slavery was a passionate topic and would prove to be a fatal issue

IV. Nation, Section, and Party

A. The Monroe Doctrine
1. Between 1810 and 1822, Spain's Latin American colonies rose in rebellion and established a series of independent nations
   a. In 1822, the Monroe administration became the first government to extend diplomatic recognition to the new Latin American republics
2. Fearing that Spain would try to regain its colonies, Secretary of State John Quincy Adams drafted the Monroe Doctrine
   a. No more European colonization of the New World
   b. The United States would abstain from European affairs
   c. No re-colonization

B. The Election of 1824
   1. Andrew Jackson was the only candidate in the 1824 election to have national appeal
   2. None of the four candidates received a majority of the electoral votes
      a. Fell to the House of Representatives
      b. Henry Clay supported John Quincy Adams
   3. Clay's "corrupt bargain" gave Adams the White House
      a. Democratic party
      b. Whig party

C. The Nationalism of John Quincy Adams
   1. John Quincy Adams enjoyed one of the most distinguished pre-presidential careers of any American president
   2. Adams had a clear vision of national greatness
      a. Supported the American system
      b. Wished to enhance American influence in the Western Hemisphere
   3. Adams held a view of federal power far more expansive than most of his contemporaries
      a. Stated that "liberty is power"
   4. His plans alarmed many and his vision would not be fulfilled until the twentieth century

D. Martin Van Buren and the Democratic Party
   1. Adams's program handed his political rivals a powerful weapon
      a. individual liberty
      b. states rights
      c. limited government
   2. Martin Van Buren viewed political party competition as a necessary and positive influence to achieve national unity

E. The Election of 1828
   1. By 1828, Van Buren had established the political apparatus of the Democratic party
   2. Andrew Jackson campaigned against John Quincy Adams in 1828
   3. Victory went to Jackson and American politics had been transformed

V. The Age of Jackson

A. The Party System
   1. Politics had become a spectacle
   2. Party machines emerged
      a. "spoils system"
   3. National conventions chose candidates

B. Democrats and Whigs
   1. Democrats and Whigs approached issues that emerged from the market revolution differently
   2. Democrats favored nongovernment intervention in the economy
   3. Whigs supported government promotion of the economy

C. Public and Private Freedom
   1. The party battles of the Jacksonian era reflected the clash between "public" and "private" definitions of American freedom and their relationship to governmental power
   2. Democrats supported a weak federal government, championing individual and states' rights
      a. Reduced expenditures
      b. Reduced tariffs
      c. Abolished the national bank
   3. Democrats opposed attempts to impose a unified moral vision on society
   4. Whigs believed that a strong federal government was necessary to promote liberty
   5. Whigs argued that the role of government was to promote the welfare of the people
D. The Nullification Crisis
   1. Jackson's first term was dominated by a battle to uphold the supremacy of federal over state law
      a. Tariff of 1828
   2. South Carolina led the charge for a weakened federal government
   3. John C. Calhoun emerged as the leading theorist of nullification
      a. Exposition and protest
         i. States created the Constitution
   4. Daniel Webster argued that the people, not the states, created the Constitution
   5. Calhoun and Jackson disagreed about the meaning of liberty and union and nullification
      a. Calhoun left the Democratic party for the Whigs
E. Indian Removal
   1. The expansion of cotton and slavery forced the relocation of Indians
      a. Indian Removal Act of 1830
      b. Five Civilized Tribes
   2. The law marked a repudiation of the Jeffersonian idea that "civilized" Indians could be assimilated into the American population
   3. The Cherokees went to court to protect their rights
      a. *Cherokee Nation v. Georgia*
      b. *Worcester v. Georgia*
   4. John Ross led Cherokee resistance
      a. Trail of Tears
   5. The Seminoles fought a war against removal
   6. William Apess appealed for harmony between white Americans and Indians

VI. The Bank War and After
  A. Biddle's Bank
    1. The Bank of the United States symbolized the hopes and fears inspired by the market revolution
    2. Heading the Bank was Nicholas Biddle of Pennsylvania
      a. Jackson distrusted the bank
      b. Biddle's bank threatened Jackson's reelection
    3. Jackson vetoed a bill to renew the Bank's charter
  B. The Pet Banks and the Economy
    1. Both "soft money" advocates and "hard money" advocates supported Jackson's veto
    2. Jackson authorized the removal of federal funds from the vaults of the National Bank and their deposit in local banks
      a. "pet banks"
      b. Roger Taney
    3. Prices rose dramatically but "real wages" declined
  C. The Panic of 1837
    1. By 1836 gold or silver was required by the American government and the Bank of England for payments
    2. With cotton exports declining, the United States suffered a panic in 1837 and a depression until 1843
    3. Martin Van Buren approved the Independent Treasury to deal with the crisis
    4. The Independent Treasury split the Democratic party
      a. Calhoun went back to the Democrats
  D. The Election of 1840
    1. The Whigs nominated William Henry Harrison in 1840
    2. Harrison was promoted as the "log cabin" candidate
      a. Running mate was John Tyler
    3. Selling candidates in campaigns was as important as the platform for which they stood
  E. His Accidency
    1. Harrison died a month after taking office
    2. Tyler vetoed measures to enact the American System

SUGGESTED DISCUSSION QUESTIONS

- Discuss how, during the Age of Jackson, politics became a spectacle.
- Describe how Andrew Jackson embodied the prevailing mood of America. What did Americans see in his life and character that made him so popular?
- Discuss the ways liberty and freedoms were used to justify the removal of the Indians in the 1830s. How did opponents to Indian removal use liberty and freedom?

- How did the nullification crisis illustrate the divide between North and South? Compare the significance of the nullification crisis with the Missouri Compromise.
- How were "liberty" and "freedom" used by various sides of the debate over the bank war?
- Women and blacks were left out of the political democracy. These two groups were also left out of the market revolution. Was it inevitable that their exclusion from one would lead to their exclusion from the other? What determined their exclusion?

SUPPLEMENTAL WEB AND VISUAL RESOURCES

The Panic of 1819

www.mises.org/rothbard/panic1819.pdf

This site is an essay in PDF format prepared by the Ludwig von Mises Institute in 2002. It covers the Panic of 1819 with the reactions and policies that accompanied it.

The Monroe Doctrine

www.wikipedia.org/wiki/Monroe_Doctrine

This free encyclopedia site includes many links to additional material related to the Monroe Doctrine.

The Indian Removal Act of 1830

www.studyworld.com/indian_removal_act_of_1830.htm

This Studyworld Web site has a wealth of knowledge including the document and a critique of the Indian Removal Act of 1830.

Indian Removal

www.pbs.org/wgbh/aia/part4/4p2959.html

This PBS resource bank is part of a larger focus on Africans in America. Indian removal is a specific focus.

Trail of Tears

www.pbs.org/weta/thewest/program/episodes/two/trailtears.htm

From the PBS series *The West* by Ken Burns, volume two, "Trail of Tears," concentrates on the Indian Removal Act of 1830.

SUPPLEMENTAL PRINT RESOURCES

Feller, Daniel. "Politics and Society: Toward a Jacksonian Synthesis." *Journal of the Early Republic* 10, no. 2 (1990): 135–61.

Perdue, Theda. *Cherokee Women: Gender and Culture Change, 1700–1835.* Lincoln: University of Nebraska Press, 1998.

Remini, Robert. *Henry Clay: Statesman for the Union.* New York: Norton, 1991.
Silbey, Joel. *Martin Van Buren and the Emergence of American Popular Politics.* Lanham, MD: Rowman & Littlefield, 2002.
Watson, Harry. *Andrew Jackson vs. Henry Clay: Democracy and Development in Antebellum America.* New York: Bedford, 1998.
Weeks, William Earl. *John Quincy Adams & American Global Empire.* Louisville: University of Kentucky Press, 1992.

TEST BANK

Matching

d	1. Thomas Dorr	a. Missouri Compromise author
i	2. Henry Clay	b. Second Bank of the United States
f	3. John Calhoun	c. Cherokee resistance leader
h	4. Albert Gallatin	d. temporary Rhode Island governor
a	5. James Tallmadge	e. senator who denounced nullification as treasonous
c	6. John Ross	f. advocate and theorist behind nullification
e	7. Daniel Webster	g. advocated a powerful federal government as president
g	8. John Quincy Adams	h. Jefferson's treasury secretary
j	9. Martin Van Buren	i. accused of making a "corrupt bargain"
b	10. Nicholas Biddle	j. founder of the Democratic Party

h	1. Missouri Compromise	a. Bank of the United States was constitutional
d	2. "corrupt bargain"	b. America's diplomatic declaration of independence
a	3. *McCulloch v. Maryland*	c. opposed Andrew Jackson
e	4. minstrels	d. election of 1824
c	5. Whig party	e. performers in racist theatrical shows
i	6. American System	f. movement against alcohol
b	7. Monroe Doctrine	g. getting a job based on party loyalty, not merit
j	8. Force Bill	h. maintained the balance of power between slave and free states
f	9. temperance	i. political program for economic development
g	10. spoils system	j. authorized use of the military to collect customs duties

Multiple Choice

1. Andrew Jackson's inauguration
   a. was small and dignified
   b. was much like the previous presidential inaugurations
   c. was limited to only the upper-crust of society
   *d. was a large, rowdy event
   e. was a disastrous affair since Jackson's opponents protested outside the White House

2. The Dorr War was
   a. caused by an argument between John Quincy Adams and Andrew Jackson
   b. between Georgians and Cherokees
   c. was an example of how contentious the national bank debate was
   *d. an exception to the trend of democratization
   e. the result of the nullification crisis

3. By 1840, approximately _____ percent of adult white men were eligible to vote.
   a. 50
   b. 60
   c. 70
   d. 80
   *e. 90

4. A primary reason that both women and blacks were excluded from the expansion of democracy was because
   a. it was reasoned that since they did not have the vote in England, they ought not to have the vote in America
   b. neither group were citizens, so the vote could not be extended to them
   *c. both groups were viewed as being naturally incapable and thus unfit for suffrage
   d. neither group had asked to be included in politics
   e. both groups were largely illiterate, which was a necessary skill for political participation

5. Which part of the American System proved to be the most controversial?
   a. a new national bank
   b. establishment of a permanent army
   *c. federal financing of improved roads and canals
   d. income tax
   e. tariff policy

6. What did the Second Bank of the United States do?
   a. issued paper money
   b. collected taxes
   c. paid the government's debts

d. made a profit for itself
*e. all of the above

7. *McCulloch v. Maryland* ruled that
   a. the Indians were not allowed to sue the federal government
   *b. the Bank of the United States was constitutional
   c. Catholics could not be barred from political office
   d. the American System was unconstitutional
   e. states could not nullify federal laws

8. The Missouri Compromise
   a. allowed popular sovereignty in Missouri to determine if it would be a slave or free state
   b. banned slavery in all territories west of Missouri
   *c. preserved the Congressional balance between slave and free states
   d. was bitterly fought against by some Southern politicians
   e. required all Missouri slaves to be emancipated within ten years

9. Why was a second Missouri Compromise necessary?
   a. Maine's state constitution allowed slavery to continue until 1840
   *b. Missouri's state constitution barred free blacks from entering the state
   c. Henry Clay refused to vote for the first Missouri Compromise
   d. Texas wished to enter the Union as a slave state at the same time
   e. Missouri's state constitution prohibited wage-labor

10. The Monroe Doctrine
   a. allowed Maine and Missouri to enter the Union as states
   b. secured Florida from Spain
   *c. declared American abstention from European affairs
   d. made the United States a policing power in the Western Hemisphere
   e. settled the nullification crisis favorably for South Carolina

11. The "Era of Good Feelings" was a term given to
   a. an informal truce observed by northwestern fur traders and Indians after the War of 1812
   b. a period of relative calm between the United States and Great Britain
   *c. the two terms of James Monroe
   d. the ten years after the Missouri Compromise
   e. the political cooperation between the Democrats and the Whigs

12. The national plan that President John Quincy Adams had for American development included
   a. legislation promoting agriculture, commerce, and manufacturing
   b. the establishment of a national university
   c. creating a naval academy
   d. building a national astronomical observatory
   *e. all of the above

13. The national political parties of the second American party system were
    *a. Democrats and Whigs
    b. Republicans and Democrats
    c. Whigs and Know-Nothings
    d. Republicans and Whigs
    e. Democrats and Federalists

14. The practice of giving a political office to someone based on loyalty to the Party is called
    a. a meritocracy
    *b. spoils system
    c. paternalism
    d. Party system
    e. nepotism

15. Which statement about the Whigs is false?
    a. They believed that the government ought to promote the economy
    b. They were established as an opposition group to Andrew Jackson
    c. They supported implementation of the American System
    *d. They favored non-government intervention in the economy
    e. They had their strongest support in the Northeast

16. During Jackson's presidency, Democrats
    a. reduced expenditures
    b. lowered the tariff
    c. killed the national bank
    d. refused to use federal monies for internal improvements
    *e. all of the above

17. The nullification crisis of 1832 ended
    a. in civil war
    b. with South Carolina seceding from the Union
    c. with Jackson's resignation from office
    *d. with a compromised tariff
    e. when Daniel Webster gave a powerful speech to the Senate in favor of nullification

18. By 1827, Cherokees had their own
    a. constitution
    b. schools
    c. newspapers
    d. codes of laws
    *e. all of the above

19. The panic of 1837 was caused in part by all of the following *except*
    a. declining cotton prices
    *b. low tariffs

c. land speculation
d. the bank war
e. the Specie Circular

20. The log cabin candidate was
a. John Quincy Adams
b. Henry Clay
c. Martin Van Buren
*d. William Henry Harrison
e. Andrew Jackson

True or False

T 1. The French writer Alexis de Tocqueville identified democracy as an essential attribute of American freedom.

F 2. Women enjoyed an expansion of democratization for themselves, as they were welcomed into the public sphere.

F 3. Since President Madison believed that a constitutional amendment was necessary for the government to build roads ands canals, the Twelfth Amendment was passed by Congress and ratified to the Constitution in 1816.

F 4. Since the Bank of the United States handled the Panic of 1819 so efficiently, public support for the banking system increased dramatically.

T 5. James Monroe's two terms as president were characterized by the absence of two-party competition.

F 6. The Missouri Compromise debate illustrated that northern Republicans did not want slavery to expand for moral reasons.

F 7. The Monroe Doctrine was a forceful statement that declared that westward expansion for the United States could not be prevented on any account since its destiny was divinely appointed.

T 8. Andrew Jackson was the only candidate in the 1824 election to have national appeal.

F 9. John C. Calhoun's "corrupt bargain" gave John Quincy Adams the White House in 1824.

T 10. Martin Van Buren believed that party politics was an important component in ensuring liberty for the American people.

T 11. The election of 1828 witnessed a campaign that compared John Quincy Adams's education to Andrew Jackson's military career.

F 12. Andrew Jackson's vision of democracy excluded blacks, but included Indians.

T 13. The "Kitchen Cabinet" was an informal group of advisers who helped to write speeches for Andrew Jackson.

T 14. The party battles of the Jacksonian era reflected the clash between "public" and "private" definitions of American freedom and their relationship to governmental power.

F 15. Andrew Jackson's policies resulted in a higher national debt.

T 16. Whigs believed that the federal government was responsible for promoting the welfare of the people and securing liberty.

T 17. Supporters of nullification cried that the federal government was overstepping its rights and infringing upon states' liberty.

F 18. Daniel Webster insisted that the national government had been created by an agreement among sovereign states, each of which retained the right to prevent the enforcement within its borders of acts of Congress that exceeded the powers specifically spelled out in the document.

F 19. The Trail of Tears was the removal of the Seminole Indians from Florida to present-day Oklahoma.

T 20. The Independent Treasury completely separated the federal government from the nation's banking system.

Short Answer

Identify and give the historical significance of each of the following terms, events, and people in a paragraph or two.

1. Panic of 1837
2. American System
3. Whig party
4. Democratic party
5. John Quincy Adams
6. Missouri Compromise
7. nullification crisis
8. Indian Removal Act
9. Nicholas Biddle
10. spoils system

Essay Questions

1. A delegate to the 1837 Pennsylvania convention remarked that the political community was based upon white persons. In this age of expanding political participation, analyze how and why some segments of the population were able to achieve greater liberties, while others were excluded. What arguments did each group make for a greater political voice? Be sure to address the *Voices of Freedom* document in your answer.

2. Describe John Quincy Adams's dream for the United States as secretary of state and as president. What role did he wish the federal government to play? How did his vision for America expand liberties or freedom? How did it restrict liberties or freedom?
3. The admittance of Missouri to the Union sparked a national crisis. Describe the debates that led up to the final compromise. How does the Missouri Compromise illustrate that sectional issues would surely arise again?
4. Fully explain how Andrew Jackson's confidence and personal achievements from a humble background epitomized the American people's collective spirit and personality and their belief in liberty. Your essay should capture the energy of the Age of Jackson.
5. Explain how Democrats and Whigs viewed liberty and the role of government in securing liberty.
6. Analyze the arguments that were presented during the nullification crisis. Be sure to comment on how Daniel Webster and John C. Calhoun interpreted the Constitution differently and how each defined liberty and the rights of states. Finally, speak to how the crisis illustrated the growing sectional differences in America.
7. Thinking back to previous chapters, analyze America's Indian policies up through the Indian Removal Act of 1830. Comment on Thomas Jefferson's remarks that indicated that Indian assimilation would guarantee their liberties and freedoms. Did assimilation help the Cherokees? How did the court system work for the Indians?
8. Compare the economic policies of the American System with those of Alexander Hamilton. What was similar? What was different? How do you think Hamilton would have rated presidents like John Quincy Adams and Andrew Jackson?

CHAPTER 11 The Peculiar Institution

This chapter concentrates on the history of slavery in the Old South, roughly between 1830 and 1860. The chapter begins by exploring the economic dominance of cotton in the South and how the northern and international textile industry depended upon the raw material. As the North industrialized, the South's economy rested overwhelmingly upon the cash crop of cotton. The different classes in the South are thoroughly discussed, explaining that although most white southerners did not own slaves, slavery was largely supported by the "plain folk." The various proslavery arguments are explained, illustrating how the definition of freedom was bent to justify the "peculiar institution." Southerner and proslavery advocate John C. Calhoun is featured in *Voices of Freedom,* arguing that slavery formed the foundation "on which to rear free and stable political institutions." Masters had a variety of tools to maintain order. Among them, physical violence was the most dramatic, but the threat of sale was the most effective. Slave society and culture is compared and contrasted to the society and culture of the southern free blacks. Slave culture demonstrated that slaves were able to maintain a semi-independence and self-respect via family life, folklore, and religion. Slave culture also cultivated a strong will for freedom. The chapter concludes with a look at various forms of slave resistance, from silent sabotage to full-scale rebellions.

CHAPTER OUTLINE

I. Frederick Douglass

II. The Old South
  A. Cotton Is King
    1. Strength of slavery rested on cotton
    2. Cotton industry

a. Three-fourths of the world's cotton supply came from southern United States
b. Cotton supplied textile mills in the North and Great Britain
c. Cotton represented America's biggest export

B. Slavery and the Nation
1. The North was not immune to slavery
a. Northern merchants and manufactures participated in the slave economy and shared in its profits
b. Slavery shaped the lives of all Americans
2. Southern economic growth was different from that in the North
a. There were few large cities in the South
b. The cities were centers for gathering and shipping cotton
c. The region produced less than 10 percent of the nation's manufactured goods

C. Plain Folk of the Old South
1. Three out of four white southerners did not own slaves
2. Most white southerners lived on self-sufficient farms in isolated areas and were poorly educated
3. Most supported slavery
a. A few, like Andrew Johnson and Joseph Brown, spoke out against the planter elite
b. Most white southerners supported the planter elite and slavery because of shared bonds of regional loyalty, racism, and kinship ties

D. The Planter Class
1. In 1850, the majority of slaveholding families owned five or fewer slaves
2. Fewer than 2,000 families owned 100 slaves or more
3. Ownership of slaves provided the route to wealth, status, and influence
4. Slavery was a profit-making system
a. Men watched the world market for cotton, invested in infrastructure, and managed their plantations
b. Plantation mistresses cared for sick slaves, oversaw the domestic servants, and supervised the plantation when the master was away
5. Southern slaveowners spent much of their money on material goods

E. The Paternalist Ethos
1. Southern slaveowners were committed to a hierarchical, agrarian society
2. Paternalism was ingrained in slave society
3. Southern men often dueled as part of a code of honor
4. Southern women were often trapped in a "domestic circle" of loneliness

F. The Proslavery Argument
1. Fewer and fewer southerners believed that slavery was a necessary evil

2. Proslavery argument rested on a number of pillars, including a commitment to white supremacy, biblical sanction of slavery, and historical precedent in that slavery was essential to human progress
3. Another proslavery argument held that slavery guaranteed equality for whites

G. Slavery and Liberty
1. White southerners declared themselves the true heirs of the American Revolution
2. Proslavery arguments began to repudiate the ideas in the Declaration of Independence that equality and freedom were universal entitlements
    a. John C. Calhoun believed that the language in the Declaration of Independence was indeed dangerous
3. Southern clergymen argued that submission of inferior to superior was a "fundamental law"
4. George Fitzhugh, a Virginia writer, argued that "universal liberty" was the exception, not the rule, and that slaves, because they were not burdened with financial concerns, were the happiest and freest people in the world
5. Abraham Lincoln observed that the proslavery arguments were functioning to serve only the interests of slave owners, who reaped the greatest benefit from the institution
6. By 1830, southerners defended slavery in terms of liberty and freedom—without slavery, freedom was not possible

III. Life under Slavery

A. Slaves and the Law
1. Slaves were considered property and had few legal rights
2. Slaves were not allowed to testify against a white person, carry a firearm, leave the plantation without permission, learn how to read or write, or gather in a group without a white person present, although some of these laws were not always vigorously enforced
3. Masters also controlled whether a slave married and how they spent their free time
4. Celia killed her master while resisting a sexual assault
    a. Celia was charged with murder and sentenced to die, but she was pregnant and her execution was delayed until she gave birth, so as not to deny the master his property right
5. Some laws protected slaves against mistreatment
    a. American slaves as compared to their counterparts in the West Indies and Brazil enjoyed better diets, lower infant mortality, and longer life expectancies
    b. Reasons for the above include the "paternalistic" ethos of the South, the lack of malaria and yellow fever in the South, and the high costs of slaves

6. Improvements in the slaves' living conditions were meant to strengthen slavery, not undermine it

B. Free Blacks in the Old South
   1. By 1860, there were nearly a half million free blacks in the United States and most of them lived in the South
   2. Free blacks were not all that free
      a. Free blacks were allowed by law to own property, marry, and could not be bought or sold
      b. Free blacks were not allowed by law to own a firearm, dog, or liquor. They could not testify in court or serve on a jury. They could not strike a white person, even in self-defense
   3. Unlike in Brazil or the West Indies, free blacks in the Old South enjoyed little respect or prosperity, with only a few exceptions
   4. The majority of free blacks who lived in the Lower South resided in cities like New Orleans and Charleston, while those living in the Upper South generally lived in rural areas, working for wages as farm laborers

C. Slave Labor
   1. Labor occupied most of a slave's daily existence
   2. There were many types of jobs a slave might perform: cutting wood for fuel for steamboats, working in mines, working on docks in seaports, laying railroad track, repairing bridges or roads, and working as skilled artisans

D. Gang Labor and Task Labor
   1. Most slaves worked in the fields
      a. It is estimated that 75 percent of the women and 90 percent of the men worked as field hands
   2. On large plantations they worked in "gangs" under the direction of the overseer, a man who was generally considered cruel by the slaves

E. Slavery in the Cities
   1. Most city slaves were servants, cooks, and other domestics
   2. Some city slaves were skilled artisans and occasionally lived on their own

F. Maintaining Order
   1. The system of maintaining order rested on force
   2. There were many tools a master had to maintain order, including whipping, exploiting divisions among slaves, incentives, and the threat of sale

IV. Slave Culture

A. The Slave Family
   1. Despite the threat of sale and the fact that marriage was illegal between slaves, many slaves did marry and created families
   2. Slave traders gave little attention to preserving family ties

3. Traditional gender roles were not followed in the fields, but during their own time, slaves did fall back on traditional gender roles
4. The family was vital to the carrying down of traditions from parent to child

B. Slave Religion
1. Black Christianity was distinctive and offered hope to the slaves
   a. Almost every plantation had its own black preacher
   b. Slaves worshipped in biracial churches
   c. Free blacks established their own churches
2. Masters viewed Christianity as another means of social control, requiring slaves to attend services conducted by white ministers
3. Many biblical stories offered hope and solace to slaves, including Exodus, David and Goliath, and Jonah and the whale

C. The Desire for Freedom
1. Slave culture rested on a sense of the unjustness of bondage and the desire for freedom
2. Slave folklore glorified the weak over the strong and their spirituals emphasized eventual liberation
3. All slaves saw the injustice of slavery—the hypocrisy of the Declaration of Independence and rhetoric of liberty heard around them only strengthened their desire for freedom

V. Resistance to Slavery

A. Forms of Resistance
1. The most common form of resistance was "silent sabotage"—breaking tools, feigning illness, doing poor work
2. Less common, but more serious forms of resistance included poisoning the master, arson, and armed assaults

B. Fugitive Slaves
1. Slaves had to follow the North Star as their guide
2. Of the estimated 1,000 slaves a year to escape, most left from the Upper South
3. In the Deep South, fugitive slaves often escaped to the southern cities, to blend in with the free black population
4. The Underground Railroad was a loose organization of abolitionists who helped slaves escape
   a. Harriet Tubman was an escaped slave who made twenty trips to Maryland, leading slaves to freedom
5. In 1839, a group of slaves collectively seized their freedom while on board the *Amistad*

C. Slave Revolts
1. 1811 witnessed an uprising on sugar plantations in Louisiana, which saw slaves marching towards New Orleans before militia captured them

2. In 1822, Denmark Vesey was charged with conspiracy and executed in South Carolina
    a. Vesey was a religious man who believed the Bible condemned slavery and who saw the hypocrisy of the Declaration of Independence
    b. The conspiracy was uncovered before Vesey could act

D. Nat Turner's Rebellion
1. In 1831, Nat Turner and his followers marched through Virginia, attacking white farm families
    a. Eighty slaves had joined Turner and sixty whites had been killed (mostly women and children), before militia put down the rebellion
    b. Turner was captured and executed
2. Turner's was the last large-scale rebellion in the South
3. Turner's rebellion sent shock waves through the South
    a. Virginia discussed emancipating its slaves, but failed to get enough votes in the House
    b. Instead of offering freedom, Virginia tightened its grip on slavery through new laws further limiting slaves' rights
4. 1831 marked a turning point for the Old South as the white southerners closed ranks and prepared to defend slavery to the end

SUGGESTED DISCUSSION QUESTIONS

- How did the North and South differ from each other? How was slavery the fundamental reason for these differences? How did each region benefit from others?
- What can the story about Celia tell us about attitudes held by white southerners toward property?
- What roles did families and religion play in the lives of slaves?
- Although slave culture grew from a need to survive in the face of bondage, it continued after emancipation. Explain why this was.
- Think back to previous discussions about the Declaration of Independence and the writing of the Constitution. Compare the meaning the founding fathers gave to "freedom" with the meaning proslavery advocates of the Old South gave to the word. What changed?
- Slaves did not just capitulate to their situation. What were some ways slaves resisted? How did they demonstrate a sense of semi-independence or self-worth? Why did masters allow some of this behavior?
- White society reacted strongly towards Nat Turner's rebellion. What were their reactions and what can they tell us about the stability of the peculiar institution in the South?

SUPPLEMENTAL WEB AND VISUAL RESOURCES

Academic Info/African-American History and Studies
www.academicinfo.net/africanam.html
Click on "slavery" under Table of Contents to get over fifty links for valuable sites on the topic.

Africans in America
www.pbs.org/wgbh/aia/home.html
Africans in America is a four-part PBS video about America's journey through slavery. Part IV: "Judgment Day, 1831–1865."

Amistad
www.tulane.edu/~amistad/
Home page of Tulane's Amistad Research Center

Anacostia Museum/Smithsonian institution
anacostia.si.edu/
Home page for the Center for African American History and Culture of the Smithsonian Institution.

Gilder Lehrman Institute of American History
vi.uh.edu/pages/mintz/gilder.htm
Gives links to firsthand accounts of slavery in America.

Harriet Tubman
www.harriettubmanstudy.org/
National Park Service Harriet Tubman Study has many links and valuable biographical and chronological information.

SUPPLEMENTAL PRINT RESOURCES

Bethel, Elizabeth Rauh. *The Roots of African-American Identity: Memory and History in Free Antebellum Communities.* New York: St. Martin's, 1997.

Cecelski, David. *The Waterman's Song: Slavery and Freedom in Maritime North Carolina.* Chapel Hill: University of North Carolina Press, 2001.

Fogel, Robert, and Stanley Engerman. *Time on the Cross: The Economics of American Negro Slavery.* New York: Norton, 1989.

Harris, J. William. *Plain Folk and Gentry in a Slave Society: White Liberty and Black Slavery in Augusta's Hinterlands.* Middletown, CT: Wesleyan University Press, 1985.

Larson, Kate Clifford. *Bound for the Promised Land: Harriet Tubman, Portrait of an American Hero.* New York: Ballantine Books, 2003.

Levine, Lawrence. *Black Culture and Black Consciousness: Afro-American Folk Thought From Slavery To Freedom.* New York: Oxford University Press, 1977.

Lichtenstein, Alex. "Coercion Had Its Limits." *Reviews in American History* 23, no. 1 (1995): 20–25.
McLaurin, Melton. *Celia: A Slave.* Athens: Georgia University of Press, 1991.

TEST BANK

Matching

e	1. Frederick Douglass	a. Southern politician who spoke against the slaveocracy
a	2. Andrew Johnson	b. led a "successful" slave rebellion in Virginia
j	3. Celia	c. favored returning the slaves of the *Amistad* to Cuba
b	4. Nat Turner	d. favored returning the slaves of the *Amistad* to Africa
h	5. John C. Calhoun	e. escaped slave who led abolitionist movement
i	6. Harriet Tubman	f. slave executed for conspiracy
d	7. John Quincy Adams	g. defended slavery as a natural part of hierarchical society
c	8. Martin Van Buren	h. outspoken proslavery politician
g	9. George Fitzhugh	i. part of an organization helping slaves escape to the North
f	10. Denmark Vesey	j. slave executed for killing her master

f	1. white gold	a. system to help slaves escape to the North
e	2. overseer	b. trickster tale
a	3. Underground Railroad	c. poor work and breakage of tools
b	4. Brer Rabbit	d. slavery
i	5. yeoman farmers	e. managed slaves in the field
j	6. Mason-Dixon line	f. cotton
c	7. silent sabotage	g. treating slaves in a fatherly manner
d	8. peculiar institution	h. working in the fields side-by-side
g	9. paternalism	i. had one or two, if any, slaves
h	10. gang labor	j. boundary line between Pennsylvania and Maryland

Multiple Choice

1. The slave population by 1860 was approximately
   a. 1 million
   b. 2 million

c. 3 million
*d. 4 million
e. 5 million

2. By 1850, approximately how many slave owners owned 200 slaves or more?
a. 50
b. 100
*c. 250
d. 500
e. 1,000

3. Who said that the language in the Declaration of Independence—that all men were created equal and entitled to liberty—was "the most false and dangerous of all political errors"?
*a. John C. Calhoun
b. Abraham Lincoln
c. Frederick Douglass
d. Denmark Vesey
e. Nat Turner

4. Approximately how much of the world's cotton supply came from the southern United States?
a. 25 percent
b. 33 percent
c. 50 percent
*d. 75 percent
e. 90 percent

5. Southern cities
a. were many
*b. served as centers for gathering and shipping cotton
c. enjoyed a vibrant immigrant population and culture
d. banned free blacks
e. all of the above

6. What reason explaining why the "plain folk" of the Old South felt a bond with the plantation elite is false?
*a. They were slaveholders too
b. They shared regional loyalty
c. They shared racist beliefs
d. They had kinship ties
e. They shared the same definitions for freedom and liberty

7. Which of the following was not used by southerners to justify their proslavery ideology?
a. the Bible
*b. the Declaration of Independence

c. a commitment to white supremacy
d. historical precedent
e. freedom itself

8. Celia was a black woman charged with a felony and sentenced to die. Her execution was postponed because
   a. as a free black, she had rights under the law
   b. the plantation mistress tried to stop the execution because she was her best domestic servant
   *c. she was pregnant
   d. President Van Buren granted a stay of execution
   e. she ran away

9. Free blacks in the South were
   *a. allowed to own property
   b. allowed to be bought and sold
   c. allowed to carry a firearm
   d. allowed to testify in court
   e. allowed to vote

10. Jumping over a broomstick was symbolic for
   a. a fugitive slave arriving in a free state
   *b. a slave marriage
   c. the birth of a slave baby
   d. surviving the Middle Passage
   e. a slave's move from the fields into the plantation house as a domestic servant

11. Which statement describing a slave family is accurate?
   *a. The slave family allowed for the transmission of slave culture from one generation to the next
   b. Traditional gender roles were the norm for slave families
   c. The fear of sale was not of great concern to the slave family
   d. The oldest woman on the plantation stood at the center of the slave community
   e. The family was seldom influenced by Christianity

12. Which of the following stories did not play a central role in black Christianity?
   a. The story of Exodus and Moses
   *b. Noah and the ark
   c. David and Goliath
   d. Jonah and the whale
   e. Daniel and the lion's den

13. There were many forms of slave resistance. The most common was
   a. rebellion

b. causing harm to the slavemaster
c. running away
*d. silent sabotage
e. suicide

14. The plantation masters had many means to maintain order among their slaves. According to the text, what was the most powerful weapon the plantation masters had?
a. requiring slaves to attend church
*b. the threat of sale
c. exploiting the divisions among slaves
d. withholding food
e. denying a marriage between two slaves

15. On the plantation, the man who was in charge of ensuring a profitable crop for the plantation master was called
a. the journeyman
b. the slave-driver
c. the chain-gang
*d. the overseer
e. the associate master

16. Historians estimate that approximately _____ slaves per year escaped to the North and Canada.
a. 500
*b. 1,000
c. 1,500
d. 2,000
e. 2,500

17. At what age was a slave permitted by law to enter the plantation labor force?
a. As soon as he/she could walk
b. five years old
c. eight years old
*d. ten years old
e. sixteen years old

18. Fugitive slaves
a. were mostly young men because women did not want to leave behind children
b. did not have maps and had to follow the North Star to freedom
c. sometimes fled to big southern cities in hopes of blending in with the free black communities
d. were most successful when they lived in the Upper South in states that bordered free states
*e. all of the above

19. Denmark Vesey's conspiracy
    *a. reflected the combination of American and African influences circulating at the time
    b. took place in 1831 and was a success
    c. reflected the belief of the conspirators that the Bible endorsed slavery
    d. was discovered, and Vesey escaped North to freedom
    e. resulted in over twenty deaths of white men, women, and children

20. Which statement about Nat Turner's Rebellion is true?
    a. Turner and his followers assaulted mostly men
    b. Less than twenty whites had been killed during the rebellion
    c. Turner escaped capture
    *d. The South was in a panic after the rebellion
    e. It occurred in Georgia

True or False

T 1. By 1860, the economic investment represented by the slave population exceeded the value of the nation's factories, railroads, and banks combined.

T 2. By 1860, most of the nation's cotton crop was grown east of the Mississippi.

F 3. Slavery did not affect northern merchants and manufacturers.

F 4. Most white southern families owned at least one slave.

T 5. Slaves had a few legal rights, but they were not well enforced.

T 6. It was illegal to teach a slave to read or write by the 1830s.

F 7. By 1850, most white southerners believed that slavery was, at best, "a necessary evil."

T 8. George Fitzhugh, a Virginian writer, believed slaves in the American South were not only very happy, but also the freest people in the world.

F 9. Free blacks in the South could testify in court and serve on juries.

F 10. Slave traders tried hard to keep slave families together.

F 11. The Underground Railroad used a system of railways to transport slaves.

T 12. Slaves working in the fields generally viewed the overseer as a cruel and heartless man.

F 13. Overall, slaves did not think much about freedom. They were content with their situation as long as their master was kind.

T 14. Despite being forbidden by law to marry, many slaves were able to create a family life on the plantation.

T 15. When not in the field, slaves observed more traditional gender roles.

F 16. As a general rule, slaveowners never allowed their slaves to listen to a white preacher in church.

T 17. Black Christianity is best described as a blend of African traditions and Christian beliefs.

F 18. Nat Turner was not a particularly religious man.

F 19. Three of the most well-known examples of slave resistance, Gabriel's and Vesey's conspiracies and Turner's Rebellion, took place in the heart of the plantation South.

T 20. After Nat Turner's Rebellion, Virginia discussed ending slavery in that state.

Short Answer

Identify and give the historical significance of each of the following terms, events, and people in a paragraph or two.

1. fugitive slaves
2. poor whites
3. the *Amistad*
4. free blacks in the Old South
5. paternalism
6. the slave family
7. Nat Turner's Rebellion
8. cotton
9. Frederick Douglass
10. Celia

Essay Questions

1. Explain as thoroughly as you can what was meant when one historian observed that "nothing escaped, nothing and no one," when referring to the pervasive influence of slavery.

2. Despite unimaginable hardships, slaves were able to maintain a sense of identity and a determination to attain freedom. Describe how slave culture aided those endeavors and drove their desire for freedom. Be sure to include African heritage, slave family life, folklore, and religious life in your response.

3. Explain the chapter's title: The Peculiar Institution. Recalling previous chapters as well, explain what made slavery peculiar in America. What were the ironies? Be sure to discuss the concept of freedom.

4. After Emancipation, a black minister claimed that "Freedom burned in the black heart long before freedom was born." Explain what he meant by this

statement and, using evidence from the textbook, evaluate the statement's validity.

5. Compare the American Old South to the plantation regions of Brazil and the Caribbean. How was slavery different or the same? How did those differences impact slave culture and the meaning of freedom?

6. For the most part, white southerners defended the "peculiar institution" whether or not they held slaves, whether they were rich or poor, and whether they lived on large plantations or small farms in Appalachia. Explain this irony. What were their proslavery arguments? What were the bonds that held "plain folk" and "planter elite" together?

7. How did masters manage their plantations? What were their various means for maintaining order? What were the divisions of labor?

8. Slave rebellions were rare, but an important form of resistance. Compare Denmark Vesey and Nat Turner. What did Vesey attempt to do? What did Turner attempt to do? How were these men similar? How did they view slavery and freedom? How did white society react to them and why?

CHAPTER 12 | An Age of Reform, 1820–1840

This chapter concentrates on the history of reform, including various communal endeavors, public institutions, abolitionism, and feminism. The chapter begins with the story of abolitionist and women's rights advocate Abby Kelley. The reform impulse is explored by looking at the nearly 100 reform communities, nearly all of which set out to reorganize society on a cooperative basis. As the reform movements took on more radical issues like prohibition, abolition, and pacifism, many Americans saw the reform impulse as an attack on their own freedom. The era also saw an increase in institution building, which was inspired by the conviction that those who passed through their doors could eventually be released to become productive, self-disciplined citizens. The chapter then examines the crusade against slavery, as it took on many forms from colonization to immediate abolition. The antislavery movement sought to reinvigorate the idea of freedom as a truly universal entitlement and, at every opportunity, black abolitionists rejected the nation's pretensions as a land of liberty. Also attempting to gain universal equality was the early women's movement. Comparing the condition of women with that of slavery was a powerful rhetorical tool used by feminists and is illustrated in Angelina Grimké's letter in *The Liberator* in this chapter's *Voices of Freedom*. The chapter concludes with the Seneca Falls Convention and with the split of the organized abolitionist movement into two wings in 1840 because of disputes over the proper role of women in antislavery work.

CHAPTER OUTLINE

I. Abby Kelley

II. The Reform Impulse
   A. Utopian Communities

1. About 100 reform communities were established in the decades before the Civil War
2. Nearly all the communities set out to reorganize society on a cooperative basis, hoping to restore social harmony to a world of excessive individualism, and to narrow the widening gap between rich and poor
   a. Socialism and communism entered the language

B. The Shakers
1. The Shakers were the most successful of the religious communities and had a significant impact on the outside world
2. Shakers believed men and women were spiritually equal
3. They abandoned private property and traditional family life
   a. celibacy

C. Oneida
1. The founder of Oneida, John Noyes, preached that he and his followers had become so perfect that they had achieved a state of complete "purity of heart," or sinlessness
2. Noyes and followers abandoned private property and traditional family life
   a. complex marriage
3. Oneida was an extremely dictatorial environment

D. Worldly Communities
1. New England transcendentalists established Brook Farm to demonstrate that manual and intellectual labor could coexist harmoniously
2. Although it was an exciting miniature university, Brook Farm failed in part because many intellectuals disliked farm labor

E. The Owenites
1. The most important secular communitarian was Robert Owen
2. Owen promoted communitarianism as a peaceful means of ensuring that workers received the full value of their labor
3. At New Harmony, Owen championed women's rights and education
4. Other short-lived secular communities included those established by Joseph Warren

F. Religion and Reform
1. Some reform movements drew their inspiration from the religious revivalism of the Second Great Awakening
2. The revivals popularized the outlook known as "perfectionism," which saw both individuals and society at large as capable of indefinite improvement
3. Under the impact of the revivals, older reform efforts moved in a new, radical direction
   a. prohibition, pacifism, and abolition

G. Reform and Its Critics
   1. To members of the North's emerging middle-class culture, reform became a badge of respectability
   2. Many Americans saw the reform impulse as an attack on their own freedom
      a. Drinking was a hotly debated issue
      b. Catholics rallied against the temperance movement

H. Reformers and Freedom
   1. The vision of freedom expressed by the reform movements was liberating and controlling at the same time

I. The Invention of the Asylum
   1. Americans embarked on a program of institution building
      a. jails
      b. poorhouses
      c. asylums
      d. orphanages
   2. These institutions were inspired by the conviction that those who passed through their doors could eventually be released to become productive, self-disciplined citizens

J. The Common School
   1. A tax-supported state public school system was widely adopted
   2. Horace Mann was the era's leading educational reformer
   3. Mann believed that education would "equalize the conditions of men"
      a. Avenue for social advancement
      b. Opportunity for character building
   4. Common schools provided career opportunities for women, but widened the divide between North and South

III. The Crusade against Slavery

A. Colonization
   1. The American Colonization Society promoted the gradual abolition of slavery and the settlement of black Americans in Africa
      a. Liberia
   2. Like Indian removal, colonization rested on the premise that America was fundamentally a white society
   3. Most African-Americans adamantly opposed the idea of colonization
      a. Insisted that blacks were Americans, entitled to the same rights enjoyed by whites

B. Militant Abolitionism
   1. A new generation of reformers demanded immediate abolition
      a. Believed that slavery was both sinful and a violation of the Declaration of Independence
   2. David Walker's *An Appeal to the Coloured Citizens of the World* was a passionate indictment of slavery and racial prejudice

C. The Emergence of Garrison
  1. The appearance in 1831 of *The Liberator*, William Lloyd Garrison's weekly journal published in Boston, gave the new type of abolitionism a permanent voice
  2. Some of Garrison's ideas were too radical, but his call for immediate abolition was echoed by many
     a. Garrison rejected colonization

D. Spreading the Abolitionist Message
  1. Abolitionists recognized the democratic potential in the production of printed material
  2. Theodore Weld helped to create the abolitionists' mass constituency
  3. He used the methods of the religious revivals and said slavery was a sin
  4. Identifying slavery as a sin was essential to replacing the traditional strategies of gradual emancipation and colonization with immediate abolition
  5. Nearly all abolitionists, despite their militant language, rejected violence as a means of ending slavery

E. Abolitionists and the Idea of Freedom
  1. Abolitionists repudiated the idea of "wage slavery" popularized by the era's labor movement
     a. Only slavery deprived human beings of their "grand central right—the inherent right of self-ownership"

F. A New Vision of America
  1. The antislavery movement sought to reinvigorate the idea of freedom as a truly universal entitlement
  2. Insisted that blacks were fellow countrymen, not foreigners or a permanently inferior caste
  3. Abolitionists disagreed over the usefulness of the Constitution
  4. Abolitionists consciously identified their movement with the revolutionary heritage
     a. The Liberty Bell

IV. Black and White Abolitionism

A. Black Abolitionists
  1. From its inception, blacks played a leading role in the antislavery movement
  2. Stowe's *Uncle Tom's Cabin* gave the abolitionist message a powerful human appeal
  3. Although the movement was racially integrated, whites relegated blacks to secondary positions
  4. Abolitionists launched legal and political battles against racial discrimination in the North

5. Black abolitionists developed an understanding of freedom that went well beyond the usage of most of their white contemporaries
   a. Attacked the intellectual foundations of racism

B. Liberty and Slavery
   1. At every opportunity, black abolitionists rejected the nation's pretensions as a land of liberty
   2. Black abolitionists articulated the ideal of color-blind citizenship
   3. Frederick Douglass on the Fourth of July

C. Slavery and Civil Liberties
   1. Abolitionism aroused violent hostility from northerners who feared that the movement threatened to disrupt the Union, interfere with profits wrested from slave labor, and overturn white supremacy
   2. Editor Elijah Lovejoy was killed by a mob while defending his press
   3. Mob attacks and attempts to limit abolitionists' freedom of speech convinced many northerners that slavery was incompatible with the democratic liberties of white Americans
   4. The fight for the right to debate slavery openly and without reprisal led abolitionists to elevate "free opinion" to a central place in what Garrison called the "gospel of freedom"

V. The Origins of Feminism

A. The Rise of the Public Woman
   1. Women were instrumental in the abolition movement
   2. The public sphere was open to women in ways government and party politics were not

B. Women and Free Speech
   1. Women lectured in public about abolition
      a. Grimké sisters
      b. Frances Wright
      c. Maria Stewart
   2. The Grimké sisters argued against the idea that taking part in assemblies, demonstrations, and lectures was unfeminine
      a. *Letters on the Equality of the Sexes* (1838)
         i. equal pay for equal work

C. Women's Rights
   1. Elizabeth Cady Stanton and Lucretia Mott organized the Seneca Falls Convention of 1848
      a. Raised the issue of women's suffrage for the first time
   2. The Declaration of Sentiments condemned the entire structure of inequality

D. Feminism and Freedom
   1. Lacking broad backing at home, early feminists found allies abroad
   2. Women deserved the range of individual choices, the possibility of self-realization, that constituted the essence of freedom

3. Margaret Fuller sought to apply to women the transcendentalist idea that freedom meant a quest for personal development

E. Women and Work
1. The participants at Seneca Falls rejected the identification of the home as women's "sphere"
   a. the "bloomer" costume
2. The movement posed a fundamental challenge to some of their society's central beliefs

F. The Slavery of Sex
1. The concept of the "slavery of sex" empowered the women's movement to develop an all-encompassing critique of male authority and their own subordination
2. Marriage and slavery became a powerful rhetorical tool for feminists

G. "Social Freedom"
1. The demand that women should enjoy the rights to regulate their own sexual activity and procreation and to be protected by the state against violence at the hands of their husbands challenged the notion that claims to justice, freedom, and individual rights should stop at the household's door
2. The issue of women's private freedom revealed underlying differences within the movement for women's rights

H. The Abolitionist Schism
1. When organized abolitionism split into two branches in 1840, the immediate cause was a dispute over the proper role of women in antislavery work
   a. American Antislavery Society
   b. American and Foreign Antislavery Society
2. The Liberty Party was established in hopes of making abolitionism a political movement

SUGGESTED DISCUSSION QUESTIONS

- To what were the newly established communal and utopian communities reacting? What was it about society that made these group members attempt to create alternative lifestyles?
- Discuss how the vision of freedom expressed by the reform movements was liberating and controlling at the same time.
- Explain how public school was supposed to "equalize the conditions of men."
- How does the life of Abby Kelley reflect the many reform impulses of antebellum America?
- Discuss what role blacks played in the abolition movement.

- Describe the various proposals involving the crusade against slavery. For example, who was in favor of colonization? Who was against it? Who favored immediate abolition?
- Compare slavery with the condition of women in antebellum America. Was it fair when feminists used slavery as a rhetorical tool for their cause?

SUPPLEMENTAL WEB AND VISUAL RESOURCES

The Shakers
religiousmovements.lib.virginia.edu/nrms/Shakers.html
This University of Virginia Web site focuses on the religious culture of the Shakers.

David Walker
www.pbs.org/wgbh/aia/part4/4p2930.html
PBS has a special online resource called "Africans in America" with an excerpt on David Walker, one of the proponents of abolitionism.

Uncle Tom's Cabin
www.films.com/Films_Home/item.cfm?s=1&bin=933
A video resource provided by Films for the Humanities and Sciences.

Transcendentalists
womenshistory.about.com/library/weekly/aa032299.htm
The History Net has a special focus on transcendentalists with a variety of articles and information on the women of that group.

Letters on the Equality of the Sexes
www.pinn.net/~sunshine/book-sum/grimke3.html
This extensive Web site contains various letters written by the Grimké sisters.

SUPPLEMENTAL PRINT RESOURCES

Ginzberg, Lori. *Women in Antebellum Reform*. Wheeling, IL: Harlan Davidson, 2000.

Hamm, Thomas. *God's Government Begun: The Society for Universal Inquiry and Reform, 1842–1846*. Bloomington: Indiana University Press, 1996.

Horton, James Oliver, and Lois Horton. *In Hope of Liberty: Culture, Community, and Protest Among Northern Free Blacks, 1700–1860*. New York: Oxford University Press, 1997.

Jeffrey, Julie Roy. *The Great Silent Army of Abolitionism: Ordinary Women in the Antislavery Movement*. Chapel Hill: University of North Carolina Press, 1998.

Wellman, Judith "The Seneca Falls Women's Rights Convention: A Study of Social Networks." *Journal of Women's History* 3, no. 1 (1991): 9–37.

TEST BANK

Matching

f	1. Dorothea Dix	a. equated slavery with sin
j	2. Sarah Grimké	b. *The Liberator*
b	3. William L. Garrison	c. *Uncle Tom's Cabin*
i	4. Elijah Lovejoy	d. New Harmony
g	5. Horace Mann	e. organized the Seneca Falls Convention
h	6. David Walker	f. advocate for the mentally ill
e	7. Elizabeth Cady Stanton	g. leading educational reformer
a	8. Theodore Weld	h. *An Appeal to the Coloured Citizens of the World*
d	9. Robert Owen	i. editor and first martyr of the abolitionist movement
c	10. Harriet Beecher Stowe	j. *Letters on the Equality of the Sexes*

h	1. burned over districts	a. made abolition a political movement
i	2. gag rule	b. group of reformed drinkers
f	3. common schools	c. Seneca Falls Convention
g	4. temperance	d. New England transcendentalists
a	5. the Liberty Party	e. advocated blacks returning to Africa
d	6. Brook Farm	f. tax-supported public schools
c	7. Declaration of Sentiments	g. movement against alcohol
j	8. "bloomer" costume	h. area of intensive revivals in NY and Ohio
e	9. American Colonization Society	i. preventing petitions to be heard in Congress
b	10. Washingtonian Society	j. feminist style of dress

Multiple Choice

1. Who gave more speeches and traveled more miles than any other female orator during the antebellum period?
   a. Lucy Stone
   *b. Abby Kelley
   c. Elizabeth Cady Stanton
   d. Lucretia Mott
   e. Angelina Grimké

2. About _____ reform communities were established in the decades before the Civil War.
   a. 20
   b. 50
   *c. 100
   d. 200
   e. 500

3. Nearly all the reform communities
   a. set out to reorganize society on a cooperative basis
   b. hoped to restore social harmony to a world of excessive individualism
   c. tried to narrow the widening gap between rich and poor
   d. did not observe traditional gender relations
   *e. all of the above

4. Which statement about Shakers is false?
   a. They adopted orphans
   b. They were successful economically
   *c. They practiced "complex marriage" and recorded sexual relations in a public record book
   d. They believed that men and women were spiritually equal
   e. They abandoned private property and traditional family life

5. Robert Owen's community New Harmony
   *a. championed women's rights and education
   b. did not allow women to get a divorce
   c. was the most successful religious reform community
   d. set up "phalanxes"
   e. fostered a dictatorial environment

6. The American Temperance Society was established in 1826 and, by 1840,
   a. Americans were consuming more beer, but less hard liquor
   b. it had disbanded
   c. it had succeed in achieving a national prohibition law
   d. there was no change in Americans' drinking habits
   *e. consumption of alcohol per person had fallen substantially

7. In the antebellum era, Americans embarked on a program of institution building, producing
   a. jails
   b. poorhouses
   c. asylums
   d. orphanages
   *e. all of the above

8. The proliferation of new institutions during the antebellum era demonstrated
   a. the lengths to which the federal government was going in order to provide for the general well-being of its citizens

b. the power of the Whig Party
*c. the tension between liberation and control in the era's reform movements
d. the expansion of liberty for those members of society who could not take care of themselves
e. the general economic prosperity of the nation

9. Horace Mann believed that public schools
   a. would "equalize the conditions of men"
   b. were an avenue for social advancement
   c. provided an opportunity for character building
   d. provided career opportunities for women
   *e. all of the above

10. The American Colonization Society promoted the gradual abolition of slavery and the settlement of black Americans to
   a. the West
   b. South Africa
   c. northern cities
   *d. Liberia
   e. the West Indies

11. The author of *An Appeal to the Coloured Citizens of the World*, David Walker, was
   a. a white northern politician
   b. a slave who smuggled his manuscript out via the Underground Railroad
   *c. a free black who operated a business in Boston
   d. a free black from Bermuda
   e. a southern white activist who believed slavery was immoral

12. William Lloyd Garrison published an abolitionist newspaper called
   a. *The Free Press*
   *b. *The Liberator*
   c. *The Abolitionist*
   d. *North Star*
   e. *Freedom*

13. William Lloyd Garrison argued in *Thoughts on African Colonization* that
   a. blacks could never fully achieve equality in America and would be happier in Africa
   b. because slaves were uneducated, it was necessary to educate them in America before sending them to Africa
   *c. blacks were not "strangers" in America to be shipped abroad, but rather they were already part of American society and should stay
   d. colonization was an expensive proposal that needed to be subsidized through a tax on cotton
   e. because blacks had no political experience, Garrison himself ought to be appointed governor of the African colony

14. If William Lloyd Garrison was the antislavery movement's most notable propagandist, _____ helped to create its mass constituency.
    a. David Walker
    *b. Theodore Weld
    c. Abby Kelley
    d. Charles Finney
    e. Lydia Maria Child

15. What did the Fourth of July represent to Frederick Douglass?
    *a. the hypocrisy of a nation that proclaimed liberty, but sanctioned slavery
    b. the ultimate celebration of freedom
    c. a beacon of hope that some day America would honor the proclamation that "all men are created equal"
    d. an opportunity for slaves to join in a mass rebellion against their masters
    e. the anniversary of his freedom, after running away from his master

16. The "gag rule"
    a. stated that newspapers could not print antislavery materials
    *b. prevented Congress from hearing antislavery petitions
    c. was applied to John Quincy Adams when he spoke about emancipation
    d. prevented Congregational ministers from preaching against Catholics
    e. was adopted at the Seneca Falls Convention to symbolize that women do not have a voice in politics

17. Dorothea Dix devoted her life to the crusade for
    a. the immediate abolition of slavery
    b. the establishment of common schools in the South
    c. the better treatment of convicted criminals in jail
    *d. the construction of humane mental hospitals for the insane
    e. the right for women to vote in local school elections

18. At the Women's Rights Convention at Seneca Falls, New York,
    a. participants endorsed the concept of a women's "sphere"
    b. participants embraced abolitionism as the official policy for their organization
    c. participants voted to petition Congress for an Equal Rights Amendment
    d. participants agreed that the right to vote was not necessary for women
    *e. participants wished to have greater access to education and employment

19. Which group of people took the concept of "social freedom" as their own, greatly expanding its meaning?
    a. abolitionists
    *b. feminists
    c. slaves
    d. wage workers
    e. transcendentalists

20. The _____ was established in hopes of making abolitionism a political movement.
    *a. the Liberty Party
    b. the Whig Party
    c. the North Star Party
    d. the Republican Party
    e. the African-American Party

True or False

T 1. The Shakers were the most successful of the religious reform communities and had a significant impact on the outside world.

F 2. All of the reform communities shared a completely democratic system.

T 3. Although it was an exciting miniature university, the transcendentalists' Brook Farm community failed in part because many of the intellectuals who participated disliked farm labor.

T 4. To members of the North's emerging middle-class culture, reform became a badge of respectability.

F 5. In general, Catholics supported the temperance movement.

T 6. Institutions like jails, mental hospitals, and public schools were inspired by the conviction that those who passed through their doors could eventually be released to become productive, self-disciplined citizens.

F 7. By 1860, every state except two had established tax-supported school systems.

F 8. Both the reform communities and the institutional movements were chiefly a phenomenon of the South.

F 9. Most African-Americans enthusiastically favored the colonization idea and returning to Africa.

T 10. Nearly all abolitionists, despite their militant language, rejected violence as a means of ending slavery.

T 11. Abolitionists were among the first to appreciate the key role of public opinion in a mass democracy, focusing their efforts on awakening the nation to the moral evil of slavery.

F 12. Abolitionists agreed with the labor movement's argument that workers really were subjugated to "wage slavery."

T 13. Abolitionists consciously identified their movement with the revolutionary heritage.

T 14. Black abolitionists developed an understanding of freedom that went well beyond the usage of most of their white contemporaries.

T 15. Mob attacks and attempts to limit abolitionists' freedom of speech convinced many northerners that slavery was incompatible with the democratic liberties of white Americans.

F 16. As women began to take an active role in abolition, public speaking for women became acceptable.

F 17. Dorothea Dix devoted her life to the cause of temperance, founding the American Temperance Organization.

F 18. The participants at Seneca Falls embraced the identification of the home as women's "sphere."

T 19. The demand that women should enjoy the rights to regulate their own sexual activity and procreation and to be protected by the state against violence at the hands of their husbands challenged the notion that claims to justice, freedom, and individual rights should stop at the household's door.

T 20. The abolitionist movement split into two in part because Abby Kelley had been appointed to an office within the American Antislavery Society, which angered some men who believed it was wrong for women to occupy such a prominent position.

Short Answer

Identify and give the historical significance of each of the following terms, events, and people in a paragraph or two.

1. Abby Kelley
2. William Lloyd Garrison
3. institution building
4. Shakers
5. Oneida
6. common schools
7. American Colonization Society
8. Grimké sisters
9. Declaration of Sentiments
10. Elijah Lovejoy

Essay Questions

1. The various reform communities that sprung up throughout America typically understood the meaning of freedom differently from mainstream Americans. Analyze the various meanings these groups gave to the word "freedom" and compare them with those of mainstream America. Your essay ought to give the reader a sense of what these communities were rejecting about mainstream society.

2. Abolitionists' greatest achievement lay in shattering the conspiracy of silence that had sought to preserve national unity by suppressing public debate over slavery. Explain how the abolitionists achieved this and comment on how successful the movement was, or was not.

3. Explain how the religious revivals of the Great Awakening popularized the outlook known as "perfectionism," which saw both individuals and society at large as capable of indefinite improvement, and how this potential directly inspired the establishment of the various reform movements.

4. As the reform impulse in the antebellum era progressed, the movement took on more radical issues than its predecessors. Describe the various issues that the reform movement took up and discuss why many Americans saw the reform impulse as an attack on their own freedom.

5. Describe how Theodore Weld's argument that slavery was a sin was both radical and necessary for the success of immediate abolition.

6. One of the debates within the antislavery crusade was colonization. Explain the various arguments for and against colonization.

7. Blacks viewed freedom and liberty differently than whites. Defend this statement with examples.

8. Abolitionists fought for the right to debate slavery openly and without reprisal. Analyze what led them to elevate "free opinion" to a central place in what William Lloyd Garrison called the "gospel of freedom."

9. Frederick Douglass wrote, "When the true history of the antislavery cause shall be written, women will occupy a large space in its pages." Was Douglass correct? Explain the role women played in the abolitionist movement. Then analyze how that experience influenced the feminist movement.

10. What were the women at Seneca Falls advocating? Be sure to explain how they understood freedom and liberty. What methods were the feminists using to promote their cause?

CHAPTER 13 | A House Divided, 1840–1861

This chapter concentrates on the events that led up to the Civil War. The chapter opens with the South's objection to sculptor Thomas Crawford's design for a Statue of Freedom to crown the Capitol's dome, illustrating how divisive the issue of slavery had become. Spurred by the idea of manifest destiny, westward expansion is covered with the Texas independence movement, the Oregon Trail, and the Mexican-American War. Freedom was extended to some groups, but denied to others as America consolidated its continental empire. With the new land from Mexico, slavery once again became a national political crisis as seen with the Compromise of 1850, the Fugitive Slave Act, and the Kansas-Nebraska Act. Demonstrating how important the issue of slavery had become for Congress, William Seward's statement on "The Irrepressible Conflict" is highlighted in *Voices of Freedom*. For the North, free soil became the rallying cry as its advocates saw slavery as competition to free labor. Along with the Free Soil Party, another new political party emerged, but in response to the growing immigration from Ireland. The American Party, or Know-Nothings, was fearful of the Irish Catholic immigrants. As these parties died away, the Republican Party, whose major platform was preventing the expansion of slavery, absorbed them. The chapter ends with the explosive events leading up to Southern secession, starting with the Kansas-Nebraska Act. Demonstrating its enormous impact upon national life, the Act destroyed the Whigs, split the Democrats, and unified the Republicans. The *Dred Scott* decision, the Lincoln-Douglas debates, and John Brown's raid on Harper's Ferry are highlighted, culminating in the 1860 election and the South's secession.

CHAPTER OUTLINE

I. Statue of Freedom

II. Fruits of Manifest Destiny

A. Continental Expansion
   1. In the 1840s, slavery moved to the center stage of American politics
      a. Territorial expansion
         i. Oregon and California
B. The Mormons' Plight
   1. The Mormons had been founded in the 1820s by Joseph Smith
   2. The absolute authority Smith exercised over his followers, and the refusal of the Mormons to separate church and state, alarmed many neighbors
      a. polygamy
   3. Smith's successor, Brigham Young, led his followers to Utah
C. The Mexican Frontier
   1. Mexico won its independence from Spain in 1821
      a. Northern frontier was California, New Mexico, and Texas
   2. California's non-Indian population in 1821 was vastly outnumbered by Indians
      b. Californios versus Indios
D. The Texas Revolt
   1. The first part of Mexico to be settled by significant numbers of Americans was Texas
      a. Moses Austin
   2. Alarmed that its grip on the area was weakening, the Mexican government in 1830 annulled existing land contracts and barred future emigration from the United States
      a. Stephen Austin led the call from American settlers demanding greater autonomy within Mexico
   3. General Antonio López de Santa Anna sent an army in 1835 to impose central authority
   4. Rebels formed a provisional government that soon called for Texan independence
      a. The Alamo
      b. Sam Houston
   5. Texas desired annexation into the United States, but neither Jackson nor Van Buren acted on that
E. Polk and Expansion
   1. The issue of Texas annexation was linked to slavery and affected the nominations of presidential candidates
      a. Clay and Van Buren
   2. James Polk, a Tennessee slaveholder and friend of Jackson, received the Democratic nomination
      a. supported Texas annexation
      b. supported "reoccupation" of all of Oregon
   3. Polk had four clearly defined goals
      a. reduce the tariff

b. reestablish the independent treasury system
c. settle the Oregon dispute
d. bring California into the Union
4. Polk initiated war with Mexico to get California

F. The Mexican-American War
1. Although the majority of Americans supported the war, a vocal minority feared the only aim of the war was to acquire new land for the expansion of slavery
a. Henry David Thoreau's *On Civil Disobedience*
2. Combat took place on three fronts
a. California and the "bear flag republic"
b. General Stephen Kearney and Sante Fe
c. Winfield Scott and Central Mexico
3. Treaty of Guadalupe Hidalgo, 1848

G. Race and Manifest Destiny
1. A region that for centuries had been united was suddenly split in two, dividing families and severing trade routes
a. "Male citizens" were guaranteed American rights
b. Indians were described as "savage tribes"
2. The spirit of manifest destiny gave a new stridency to ideas about racial superiority
3. "Race" in the mid-nineteenth century was an amorphous notion involving color, culture, national origin, class, and religion

H. Redefining Race
1. Mexico had abolished slavery and declared persons of Spanish, Indian, and African origin equal before the law
2. The Texas constitution adopted after independence not only included protections for slavery but denied civil rights to Indians and persons of African origin

I. Gold Rush California
1. California's gold rush population was incredibly diverse
2. The explosive population growth and fierce competition for gold worsened conflicts among California's many racial and ethnic groups
3. The boundaries of freedom in California were tightly drawn
a. The Indians were particularly hurt

III. A Dose of Arsenic

A. The Wilmot Proviso
1. Congressman David Wilmot of Pennsylvania in 1846 proposed a resolution prohibiting slavery from all territory acquired from Mexico
2. In 1848, opponents of slavery's expansion organized the Free Soil Party
a. Martin Van Buren

B. The Free Soil Appeal

1. The free soil position had a popular appeal in the North because it would limit southern power in the federal government
2. Wage earners of the North also favored the free soil movement
3. The Free Soil platform of 1848 called both for barring slavery from western territories and for the federal government to provide homesteads to settlers without cost

C. The South and the Expansion of Slavery
   1. To single out slavery as the one form of property barred from the West would be an affront to the South and its distinctive way of life
   2. The admission of new free states would overturn the delicate political balance between the sections and make the South a permanent minority

D. Crisis and Compromise
   1. 1848 was a year of revolution in Europe, only to be suppressed by counter-revolution
   2. With the slavery issue appearing more and more ominous, established party leaders moved to resolve differences between the sections
      a. The Compromise of 1850

E. The Great Debate
   1. Powerful leaders spoke for and against compromise
      a. Daniel Webster
      b. John Calhoun
      c. William Seward
   2. President Taylor died in office and Millard Fillmore secured the adoption of the Compromise

F. The Fugitive Slave Issue
   1. The Fugitive Slave Act allowed special federal commissioners to determine the fate of alleged fugitives without benefit of a jury trial or even testimony by the accused individual
   2. In a series of dramatic confrontations, fugitives, aided by abolitionist allies, violently resisted recapture
   3. The fugitive slave law also led several thousand northern blacks to flee to safety in Canada

G. The Kansas-Nebraska Act
   1. Franklin Pierce won the 1852 presidential race
   2. Stephen Douglas saw himself as the new leader of the Senate after the deaths of Calhoun, Clay, and Webster
   3. Douglas introduced a bill for statehood for Nebraska and Kansas so that a transcontinental railroad could be constructed
      a. Slavery would be settled by popular sovereignty
   4. The *Appeal of the Independent Democrats* was issued by antislavery congressmen
   5. The Kansas-Nebraska bill became law, but shattered the Democratic party's unity

    a. Whigs collapsed
    b. South was solidly Democratic
    c. Republican Party emerged to prevent the further expansion of slavery

IV. The Rise of the Republican Party
  A. The Northern Economy
    1. The rise of the Republican party reflected underlying economic and social changes
      a. Railroad network
    2. By 1860, the North had become a complex, integrated economy
    3. Two great areas of industrial production had arisen
      a. Northeastern seaboard
      b. Great Lakes region
  B. The Growth of Immigration
    1. Economic expansion fueled a demand for labor, which was met, in part, by increased immigration from abroad
      a. Ireland and Germany
      b. Settled in the northern states
    2. Numerous factors inspired this massive flow of population across the Atlantic
      a. European economic conditions
      b. American political and religious freedoms
      c. Refugees from disaster
        i. Irish potato famine
    3. The second largest group of immigrants, Germans, included a considerably larger number of skilled craftsmen than the Irish
  C. The Rise and Fall of the Know-Nothings
    1. While immigrants from England were easily absorbed, those from Ireland encountered intense hostility
      a. Catholic Church
    2. The Irish influx thoroughly alarmed many native-born Americans
      a. "Nativists" claimed the Irish posed a threat to democratic institutions
    3. Nativism emerged as a major political movement in 1854, with the sudden appearance of the American, or Know-Nothing Party
    4. All European immigrants benefited from being white
      a. suffrage
  D. The Free Labor Ideology
    1. Republicans managed to convince most northerners that the slave power posed a more immediate threat to their liberties and aspirations than "property" and immigration
      a. Appeal rested on the idea of "free labor"

2. "Free labor" could not compete with "slave labor" and so slavery's expansion had to be halted to ensure freedom for the white laborer
3. Republicans cried "freedom national"—meaning not abolition, but ending the federal government's support of slavery
   a. Republicans were not abolitionists

E. Bleeding Kansas and the Election of 1856
1. "Bleeding Kansas" seemed to discredit Douglas's policy of leaving the decision of slavery up to the local population, thus aiding the Republicans
   a. Civil War within Kansas
   b. Charles Sumner
2. The election of 1856 demonstrated that parties had reoriented themselves along sectional lines

V. The Emergence of Lincoln

A. The *Dred Scott* Decision
1. After having lived in free territories, the slave Dred Scott sued for his freedom
2. The Supreme Court justices addressed three questions
   a. Could a black person be a citizen and therefore sue in federal court?
   b. Did residence in a free state make Scott free?
   c. Did Congress possess the power to prohibit slavery in a territory?
3. Speaking for the majority, Chief Justice Roger A. Taney declared that only white persons could be citizens of the United States
4. Taney ruled that Congress possessed no power under the Constitution to bar slavery from a territory
   a. The decision in effect declared unconstitutional the Republican platform of restricting slavery's expansion

B. The Decision's Aftermath
1. Rather than abandoning their opposition to the expansion of slavery, Republicans now viewed the Court as controlled by the slave power
   a. Lecompton Constitution and Stephen Douglas

C. Lincoln and Slavery
1. In seeking reelection, Douglas faced an unexpectedly strong challenge from Abraham Lincoln
2. Although Lincoln hated slavery, he was willing to compromise with the South to preserve the Union
3. Lincoln's speeches combined the moral fervor of the abolitionists with the respect for order and the Constitution of more conservative northerners

D. The Lincoln-Douglas Campaign
1. Lincoln campaigned against Douglas for Illinois's senate seat
2. The Lincoln-Douglas debates remain classics of American political oratory
   a. To Lincoln, freedom meant opposition to slavery

    b. Douglas argued that the essence of freedom lay in local self-government and individual self-determination
  3. Lincoln shared many of the racial prejudices of his day
  4. Douglas was reelected by a narrow margin
E. John Brown at Harpers Ferry
  1. An armed assault by the abolitionist John Brown on the federal arsenal at Harpers Ferry, Virginia, further heightened sectional tensions
    a. Brown had a long career of involvement in antislavery activities
  2. Placed on trial for treason to the state of Virginia, Brown's execution turned him into a martyr to much of the North
F. The Rise of Southern Nationalism
  1. More and more southerners were speaking openly of southward expansion
    a. Ostend Manifesto
    b. William Walker and filibustering
  2. By the late 1850s, southern leaders were bending every effort to strengthen the bonds of slavery
G. The Democratic Split
  1. The Democratic party was split with its nomination of Douglas in 1860 and the southern Democrats' nomination of John Breckinridge
H. The Nomination of Lincoln
  1. Republicans nominated Lincoln over William Seward
  2. Lincoln appealed to many voters
  3. The party platform
    a. denied the validity of the Dred Scott decision
    b. opposed slavery's expansion
    c. added economic initiatives
I. The Election of 1860
  1. In effect, two presidential campaigns took place in 1860
  2. The most striking thing about the election returns was their sectional character
  3. Without a single vote in ten southern states, Lincoln was elected the nation's sixteenth president

VI. The Impending Crisis
  A. The Secession Movement
    1. Rather than accept permanent minority status in a nation governed by their opponents, Deep South political leaders boldly struck for their region's independence
    2. In the months that followed Lincoln's election, seven states stretching from South Carolina to Texas seceded from the Union
  B. The Secession Crisis
    1. President Buchanan denied that a state could secede, but also insisted that the federal government had no right to use force against it

2. The Crittenden plan was rejected by Lincoln
3. The Confederate States of America was formed on March 4, 1861
   a. Jefferson Davis as president

C. And the War Came
1. In time, Lincoln believed, secession might collapse from within
2. Lincoln also issued a veiled warning: "In your hands, my dissatisfied fellow countrymen, and not in mine, is the momentous issue of civil war"
3. After the South fired upon Fort Sumter on April 12, 1861, Lincoln called for 75,000 troops to suppress the insurrection

SUGGESTED DISCUSSION QUESTIONS

- Discuss the controversy over Thomas Crawford's Statue of Freedom.
- Discuss manifest destiny. Was westward expansion across the continent inevitable?
- What were the promises and realities of free labor?
- What destroyed the second American party system, and how was the electorate realigned?
- Why did the Compromise of 1850 fail?
- Why is it ironic that the South supported the Fugitive Slave Act?
- How did the events of the 1850s lead to the collapse of the Union in 1861? Comment on William Seward's statement in *Voices of Freedom.*
- Who was responsible for the coming of the Civil War? Was it the South's fault? The North's? Were strong personalities important? Was the war inevitable?

SUPPLEMENTAL WEB AND VISUAL RESOURCES

Manifest Destiny

www.madbbs.com/~rcw/US_History/manifest_destiny.htm

This site is a useful resource for information on the westward expansion of the United States in the 1840s.

The Mormons

www.iamoconf.xroads.net/Globetrotter3/west/mormans.htm

This site tracks the journey of the Mormons to Utah. It includes a timeline and links to other relevant material.

The Alamo

alamo-de-parras.welkin.org/history/hframe.html

This site concentrates on the historical elements of the Alamo with useful pictures and a teacher's guide.

Immigration

www.migrationinformation.org/Profiles/display.cfm?ID=6

This helpful site contains a wealth of information concerning migration in the United States with records dating back to the 1860s.

John Brown

www.shop.pbs.org/

The PBS American Experience film "John Brown's Holy War" is a 90-minute film on Brown as martyr, madman, and murderer.

Lincoln

www.films.com/Films_Home/item.cfm?s=1&bin=2024

This video portrays Lincoln's life prior to his presidency and concludes with his funeral.

SUPPLEMENTAL PRINT RESOURCES

Chaffin, Tom. *Pathfinder: John Charles Fremont and the Cause of American Empire.* New York: Hill and Wang, 2002.

Gienapp, William. "Nativism and the Creating of a Republican Majority in the North before the Civil War." *Journal of American History* 72, no. 3 (1985): 529–559.

Grimsted, David. *American Mobbing, 1828–1861: Toward Civil War.* New York: Oxford University Press, 1998.

Holt, Michael. *The Rise and Fall of the American Whig Party: Jacksonian Politics and the Onset of the Civil War.* New York: Oxford University Press, 1999.

Karsten, Peter. "Labor's Sorrow? Workers, Bosses, and the Courts in Antebellum America." *Reviews in American History* 21, no. 2 (1993): 447–453.

Majewski, John. *A House Dividing: Economic Development in Pennsylvania and Virginia Before the Civil War.* New York: Cambridge University Press, 2000.

Morrison, Michael. *Slavery and the American West: The Eclipse of Manifest Destiny and the Coming of the Cold War.* Chapel Hill: University of North Carolina Press, 1997.

Peterson, Merrill. *John Brown: The Legend Revisited.* Richmond: University of Virginia Press, 2002.

Roberts, Brian. *American Alchemy: The California Gold Rush and Middle-Class Culture.* Chapel Hill: University of North Carolina Press, 2000.

Weeks, William Earl. *Building the Continental Empire: American Expansion from the Revolution to the Civil War.* Chicago: Ivan Dee, 1996.

Winders, Richard Bruce. *Mr. Polk's Army: The American Military Experience in the Mexican War.* College Station: Texas A&M University Press, 1997.

TEST BANK

Matching

Answer	Item	Choice
g	1. Dred Scott	a. *On Civil Disobedience*
i	2. Abraham Lincoln	b. 1848 Free Soil presidential candidate
f	3. John Fremont	c. author of the Kansas-Nebraska Act
b	4. Martin Van Buren	d. filibustering
h	5. John Brown	e. author of the Compromise of 1850
d	6. William Walker	f. California hero
a	7. Henry David Thoreau	g. a slave who sued for his freedom
j	8. John Breckinridge	h. led a raid on Harpers Ferry
c	9. Stephen Douglas	i. 1860 Republican presidential candidate
e	10. Henry Clay	j. 1860 southern Democratic presidential candidate

Answer	Item	Choice
d	1. manifest destiny	a. antislavery congressmen
h	2. Wilmot Proviso	b. suggested the United States buy or seize Cuba
g	3. Kansas-Nebraska Act	c. returned runaway slaves to their master
c	4. Fugitive Slave Act	d. America's mission to settle the West
b	5. Ostend Manifesto	e. Mexican cattle ranchers
j	6. Free Soil party	f. anti-immigrant xenophobes
i	7. Compromise of 1850	g. voided the Missouri Compromise
f	8. Know-Nothing Party	h. no slavery in land acquired by Mexico
e	9. Californios	i. California entered the Union as a free state
a	10. Appeal of the Independent Democrats	j. opponents to the expansion of slavery

Multiple Choice

1. What is the irony of Thomas Crawford's Statue of Freedom that adorns the Capitol dome?
   a. The South approved its design, despite the use of the liberty cap
   b. The North approved its design, despite the use of a slave in chains
   c. Thomas Crawford owned slaves

*d. The statue was assembled under the direction of a slave craftsman
e. It was destroyed in the first month of fighting during the Civil War

2. By 1860 approximately _____ people had braved the western trails and emigrated to Oregon and California.
   a. 50,000
   b. 100,000
   c. 200,000
   *d. 300,000
   e. 400,000

3. Which statement about the Mormons is false?
   *a. The Mormons were founded in the 1820s by Brigham Young
   b. The Mormons sought refuge in Utah, near Salt Lake
   c. Leader Joseph Smith refused to separate church and state
   d. The Mormons practiced polygamy
   e. Joseph Smith exercised an absolute authority over his followers

4. Americans were attracted to Texas in the 1820s because of the
   a. ranching opportunities for cattle
   *b. abundance of land for farming
   c. mining opportunities of silver and copper
   d. Catholic predominance of the Mexican government
   e. fact that slavery was outlawed in Mexico

5. "Fifty-four forty or fight" referred to
   a. Texas
   *b. Oregon
   c. California
   d. Mexico
   e. Kansas-Nebraska

6. James Polk had four clearly defined goals when he entered the White House. Which was not one of his goals?
   a. reduce the tariff
   *b. settle the slavery dispute
   c. settle the Oregon dispute
   d. bring California into the Union
   e. reestablish the independent treasury system

7. Who spoke out against the Mexican-American War?
   a. Zachary Taylor
   b. John C. Calhoun
   c. John Fremont
   d. John O'Sullivan
   *e. Henry David Thoreau

8. Manifest destiny included all of the following justifications for expansion except
   a. it was divinely appointed
   b. America had a duty to extend democratic principles
   *c. additional land was needed for slavery to survive
   d. the superiority of the Anglo-Saxon race
   e. the desire for more land

9. "Race" in the mid-nineteenth century was an amorphous notion involving
   a. color
   b. culture and national origin
   c. religion
   d. class
   *e. all of the above

10. Freedom in California was generally
   a. extended to all immigrants and Indians in the state
   b. more broadly defined than any other state in the Union because of its Mexican heritage
   *c. limited to whites
   d. extended to all groups except the Chinese
   e. limited extended to all groups except the Indians and Mexicans

11. The Wilmot Proviso proposed a resolution
   *a. prohibiting slavery in all territory acquired from Mexico
   b. to divide Kansas and Nebraska into states
   c. settle the Oregon dispute favorably for the United States
   d. annex Cuba in order to avoid southern secession
   e. which allowed slavery to expand into Texas and New Mexico

12. Opponents to slavery's expansion organized what political party in 1848?
   a. Whig Party
   *b. Free Soil Party
   c. Republican Party
   d. Know-Nothing Party
   e. Liberty Party

13. All of the following were provisions within the Compromise of 1850 except
   a. the slave trade would be abolished in Washington, D.C.
   *b. that Kansas and Nebraska would enter the Union as a slave and free state, respectively
   c. California would enter the Union as a free state
   d. a fugitive slave law would be enacted
   e. slavery in the rest of the territory acquired from Mexico would be decided by popular sovereignty

14. The fugitive slave law
    *a. allowed the federal government to override state and local authorities
    b. was virtually ignored by the federal government
    c. was supported by abolitionists in the North
    d. had little to no effect on the nation's politics
    e. all of the above

15. Which statement about the Kansas-Nebraska Act is false?
    a. It violated the 1820 Missouri Compromise
    b. It called for popular sovereignty in deciding slavery
    c. It was authored by Stephen Douglas
    *d. It ultimately had little impact on national life
    e. It shattered the Democratic Party's unity

16. The majority of the nearly 5 million immigrants that entered the United States between 1830 and 1860 were from
    a. England and Germany
    *b. Germany and Ireland
    c. China and Ireland
    d. Mexico and England
    e. Germany and China

17. By 1856 the Republican Party included in its membership people who were
    a. northern Whigs
    b. Free Soilers
    c. Know-Nothings
    d. antislavery Democrats
    *e. all of the above

18. What attracted voters to the Know-Nothing Party?
    a. its desire to dissolve the Missouri Compromise
    b. its move to annex Cuba for the expansion of American slavery
    c. its calls for immediate emancipation of the slaves
    d. its adherence to "free soil"
    *e. its denunciation of Roman Catholic immigrants

19. The Kansas-Nebraska Act
    a. unified the Democratic Party
    b. was a successful compromise that both states' populations accepted
    c. was opposed by John Calhoun and Henry Clay
    *d. was proposed by Stephen Douglas in hopes of building a railroad through one of the states
    e. left Congress to decide whether or not the territories would enter the Union as slave or free states

20. The Supreme Court ruling *Dred Scott v. Sanford*
    a. declared that only white persons could be citizens of the United States

b. ruled that Congress possessed no power under the Constitution to bar slavery from a territory
c. in effect declared unconstitutional the Republican platform of restricting slavery's expansion
d. ruled that temporary residence in a free state did not automatically free a slave
*e. all of the above

21. The 1860 Republican platform stated that
a. the *Dred Scott* decision was invalid
b. the Party was opposed to the expansion of slavery
c. the government ought to aid in the construction of a transcontinental railroad
d. the government ought to give free homesteads in the West
*e. all of the above

True or False

F 1. In spite of the controversy over the Statue of Freedom, Thomas Crawford refused to change his original design.

F 2. The members of the Church of Jesus Christ of Latter-Day Saints were welcomed by their neighbors in New York and Ohio.

T 3. The Texas independence movement was sparked in part because the Mexican government, alarmed that its grip on the area was weakening, annulled existing land contracts and barred future emigration from the United States in 1830.

T 4. The issue of Texas annexation was linked to slavery and affected the nominations of presidential candidates the 1840s.

F 5. Unlike previous presidents, James Polk was not a slaveholder.

F 6. The explosive population growth and competition for gold brought cooperation among California's many racial and ethnic groups as they worked together for wealth.

T 7. It is ironic that the South supported the fugitive slave law in that the law gives enormous power to the federal government, overriding local authorities, which is something that the South had traditionally opposed.

T 8. Many free blacks in the North who had escaped slavery by running away fled to Canada to avoid being caught and brought back to the South by the fugitive slave law.

F 9. The Wilmot Proviso was an attempt to annex Cuba.

F 10. The *Appeal of the Independent Democrats* was not a very effective piece of political persuasion.

T 11. The development of railroads and economic integration of the Northeast and Northwest created the groundwork for the political unification of the Republican Party.

T 12. The second largest group of immigrants arriving in America during the antebellum era was the Germans and they included a considerably larger number of skilled craftsmen than the Irish.

F 13. Nativism emerged as a major political movement in 1854, with the sudden appearance of the Liberty Party.

T 14. The free labor ideology was based on the assumption that "free labor" could not compete with "slave labor" so slavery's expansion had to be halted to ensure freedom for the white laborer.

F 15. Prior to becoming president in 1856, James Buchanan did not have much political experience.

F 16. Moderate Republicans like Abraham Lincoln supported the *Dred Scott* decision.

F 17. Stephen Douglas said during the Lincoln-Douglas debates, "A house divided against itself cannot stand. I believe this government cannot endure, permanently half slave and half free."

F 18. As a result of the fine oratory performance that he gave during the campaign debates, Abraham Lincoln defeated Stephen Douglas in the Senate race.

T 19. Abraham Lincoln won the 1860 presidential election without a single vote in ten southern states.

T 20. By the time Lincoln actually took the oath of office, seven states had already seceded from the Union.

Short Answer

Identify and give the historical significance of each of the following terms, events, and people in a paragraph or two.

1. Know-Nothing Party
2. "free labor"
3. Republican Party
4. free soil
5. John Brown
6. Bleeding Kansas
7. Lincoln-Douglas debates
8. manifest destiny
9. Mexican-American War
10. Compromise of 1850

Essay Questions

1. Did morality or economics dominate the debates over slavery in the 1850s? Explain the various arguments made for and against the expansion of slavery. Who, if anyone, was arguing for abolition?

2. Compare Andrew Jackson's America of the 1830s to Abraham Lincoln's America of the 1850s. What similarities and differences are there in terms of economics, society, and politics?

3. John O'Sullivan declared that "race" was the "key" to the "history of nations" and the rise and fall of empires. How accurate do you think that statement was? Why?

4. What did Emerson mean by "Mexico will poison us"? Was he right? Why or why not?

5. California was seen as a golden opportunity for economic freedom once gold was discovered. However, the boundaries of freedom were tightly drawn in California. Explain the expansions and limitations of freedom there.

6. Analyze the arguments of the Free Soil Party. How did its members understand freedom? How did slavery fit into their platform?

7. One German newcomer wrote that "there aren't any masters [in America], here everyone is a free agent." How accurate a statement was that? Why would a German immigrant view America as free? Do you think an Irish immigrant would feel the same way about America? Why or why not?

8. Thinking back to previous chapters, fully explain how the forces of the market revolution heightened the tension between freedom and slavery.

9. Explain how the various parties reacted to the Kansas-Nebraska Act. Be sure to discuss why the Whig Party failed, why the Democratic Party split, and why the Republican Party unified. How did each party view slavery and define freedom?

10. Using the Lincoln-Douglas debates, explore how each man viewed freedom. What can their political debates tell us about American society on the eve of the Civil War?

11. Analyze Roger Taney's decision in the case of *Dred Scott v. Sanford*. How did the ruling mirror the sectional debates that had been occurring in Congress? What consequences did the decision have on the liberties and freedoms of blacks in America?

CHAPTER 14

A New Birth of Freedom: The Civil War, 1861–1865

This chapter concentrates on the history of the American Civil War, chronicling its major battles, the coming of emancipation, and the early experiments at reconstruction. The chapter begins with the compelling story of a German immigrant who volunteered in the Union army and whose story illustrates the transformation that the war went through, from preserving the Union to ending slavery. The chapter examines how the war was both a modern and total war and the relative advantages that the North had over the South. After a series of Union defeats, Lincoln began a fundamental shift in his thinking and issued the Emancipation Proclamation. Afterward, blacks fought valiantly for the Union. The chapter then looks at the Civil War as a second American Revolution, exploring the vision Lincoln had for universal political democracy and human liberty. Lincoln's views are explored in detail within *Voices of Freedom.* The Northern economy benefited greatly from the war, while the South suffered economic crisis. Victories at Gettysburg and Vicksburg turned the tide for a Union victory, which occurred when Lee surrendered at Appomattox in April 1865. Meanwhile, experiments on the Sea Islands and Grant's "negro paradise" served as illustrations for what reconstruction might look like. Lincoln also had a plan, but was assassinated days after Lee's surrender.

CHAPTER OUTLINE

I. Marcus Spiegel

II. The First Modern War
   A. The Two Combatants
      1. The North seemed to have the advantage, but Confederate soldiers were highly motivated fighters
      2. On both sides, the outbreak of war stirred powerful feelings of patriotism

B. The Technology of War
   1. Railroads were vital to the war effort
   2. Introduction of the rifle changed the nature of combat
   3. Modern warfare included P.O.W. camps and disease
C. The Public and the War
   1. Both sides were assisted by a vast propaganda effort to mobilize public opinion
   2. The war was brought to the people via newspapers and photographs
D. Mobilizing Resources
   1. The outbreak of the war found both sides unprepared
   2. Feeding and supplying armies was a challenge for both sides
   3. Despite the North's advantages, victory on the battlefield was elusive
E. The War Begins
   1. In the East, most of the war's fighting took place in a narrow corridor between Washington and Richmond
   2. First Battle of Bull Run shattered any illusions that war was romantic
   3. George McClellan assumed command of the Union Army of the Potomac
F. The War in the East in 1862
   1. General Lee blunted McClellan's attacks in Virginia and forced him to withdraw back to the vicinity of Washington
   2. Successful on the defensive, Lee now launched an invasion of the North
      a. Antietam
      b. Union victory
   3. Fredricksburg was a massacre
G. The War in the West
   1. Ulysses S. Grant was the architect of early success in the West
   2. In February 1862, Grant won the Union's first significant victory when he captured Forts Henry and Donelson in Tennessee

III. The Coming of Emancipation
A. Slavery and the War
   1. In numbers, scale, and the economic power of the institution of slavery, American emancipation dwarfed that of any other country
   2. At the outset of the war, Lincoln invoked time-honored Northern values to mobilize public support
   3. Lincoln initially insisted that slavery was irrelevant to the conflict
B. The Unraveling of Slavery
   1. Congress adopted a resolution proposed by Senator John C. Crittenden of Kentucky, which affirmed that the Union had no intention of interfering with slavery
   2. The policy of ignoring slavery unraveled, and by the end of 1861, the military began treating escaped blacks as contraband of war

3. Blacks saw the outbreak of fighting as heralding the long-awaited end of bondage

C. Steps toward Emancipation
   1. Since slavery stood at the foundation of the southern economy, antislavery northerners insisted, emancipation was necessary to weaken the South's ability to sustain the war
   2. Throughout these months, Lincoln struggled to retain control of the emancipation issue

D. Lincoln's Decision
   1. Sometime during the summer of 1862, Lincoln concluded that emancipation had become a political and military necessity
   2. On September 22, 1862, Lincoln issued the Preliminary Emancipation Proclamation
   3. The initial northern reaction was not encouraging

E. The Emancipation Proclamation
   1. Lincoln signed the Emancipation Proclamation on January 1, 1863
   2. Despite its limitations, the Proclamation set off scenes of jubilation among free blacks and abolitionists in the North and "contrabands" and slaves in the South
   3. The Emancipation Proclamation not only altered the nature of the Civil War and the course of American history, but also represented a turning point in Lincoln's own thinking

F. Enlisting Black Troops
   1. Of the Proclamation's provisions, few were more radical in their implications than the enrollment of blacks into military service
   2. By the end of the war, over 180,000 black men had served in the Union army and 24,000 in the navy
   3. Most black soldiers were emancipated slaves who joined the army in the South

G. The Black Soldier
   1. For black soldiers, military service proved to be a liberating experience
      a. At least 130 former soldiers served in political office after the Civil War
   2. The Union navy treated black sailors generally the same as white sailors
   3. Within the army, black soldiers received treatment anything but equal to white soldiers
   4. Black soldiers played a crucial role not only in winning the Civil War, but in defining the war's consequences

IV. The Second American Revolution

A. Liberty and Union

1. The Union's triumph consolidated the northern understanding of freedom as the national norm
2. Emancipation offered proof of the progressive nature and global significance of the country's history

B. Lincoln's Vision

1. To Lincoln, the American nation embodied a set of universal ideas, centered on political democracy and human liberty
2. The Gettysburg Address identified the nation's mission with the principle that "all men are created equal"

C. From Union to Nation

1. The war forged a new national self-consciousness, reflected in the increasing use of the word "nation"—a unified political entity—in place of the older "Union" of separate states

D. Liberty in Wartime

1. Lincoln consolidated executive power and twice suspended the writ of habeas corpus throughout the entire Union for those accused of "disloyal activities"
2. After the war, the Court made it clear that the Constitution was not suspended in wartime

E. The North's Transformation

1. The North experienced the war as a time of prosperity

F. Government and the Economy

1. Congress adopted policies that promoted economic growth and permanently altered the nation's financial system
   a. The Homestead Act
   b. Land Grant College Act
2. Congress passed land grants for railroads

G. A New Financial System

1. The need to pay for the war produced dramatic changes in financial policy
   a. increased tariff
   b. new taxes on goods
   c. first income tax
   d. bonds
2. Wartime economic policies greatly benefited northern manufacturers, railroad men, and financiers
3. Taken together, the Union's economic policies vastly increased the power and size of the federal government

H. Women and the War

1. Women stepped into the workforce
2. Hundreds of thousands of northern women took part in humanitarian organizations
3. Northern women were brought into the public sphere and the war work offered them a taste of independence

I. The Divided North
   1. Republicans labeled those opposed to the war Copperheads
   2. The war heightened existing social tensions and created new ones
      a. Draft riots
      b. Labor movement

V. The Confederate Nation
   A. The Confederate President
      1. Jefferson Davis proved unable to communicate effectively the war's meaning to ordinary men and women
      2. Under Davis, the Confederate nation became far more centralized than the Old South had been
         a. King Cotton Diplomacy
   B. The Inner Civil War
      1. Social change and internal turmoil engulfed much of the Confederacy
         a. The draft
   C. Economic Problems
      1. Unlike the North, the South's economy was in crisis during the war
      2. Numerous yeoman families, many of whom had gone to war to preserve their economic independence, sank into poverty and debt
      3. By the war's end, over 100,000 Southern men had deserted
   D. Southern Unionists
      1. Southerners loyal to the Union made a significant contribution to northern victory
      2. Elizabeth Van Lew provided vital information to Union Forces
   E. Women and the Confederacy
      1. Even more than in the North, the war placed unprecedented burdens on southern white women
      2. The growing disaffection of southern white women contributed to the decline in homefront morale and encouraged desertion from the army
   F. Black Soldiers for the Confederacy
      1. A shortage of manpower led the South to arm slaves to fight
      2. The war ended before the recruitment of black soldiers actually began
   G. Gettysburg and Vicksburg
      1. Lee advanced onto Northern soil, but was held back by Union forces under the command of General George Meade
         a. Pickett's charge
      2. General Grant secured a Union victory at Vicksburg
   H. 1864
      1. Grant, in 1864, began a war of attrition against Lee's army in Virginia
      2. At the end of six weeks of fighting, Grant's casualties stood at 60,000—almost the size of Lee's entire army—while Lee had lost 25,000 men

3. General William T. Sherman entered Atlanta, seizing Georgia's main railroad center

I. The Election of 1864
   1. Republicans nominated John C. Fremont on a platform calling for a constitutional amendment to abolish slavery, federal protection of the freedmen's rights, and confiscation of the land of leading Confederates.
   2. The Democratic candidate for president was General George B. McClellan

VI. Rehearsals for Reconstruction and the End of the War
   A. The Sea Island Experiment
      1. The Union occupied the Sea Islands in November 1861
      2. Women took the lead as teachers in educating the freed slaves of the islands
         a. Charlotte Forten and Laura Towne
      3. By 1865 black families were working for wages, acquiring education, and enjoying better shelter and clothing and a more varied diet than under slavery
   B. Wartime Reconstruction in the West
      1. After the capture of Vicksburg, the Union army established regulations for plantation labor
         a. Freedmen signed labor contracts and were paid wages
      2. Neither side was satisfied with the new labor system
      3. At Davis Bend, Grant established a "negro paradise"
   C. The Politics of Wartime Reconstruction
      1. In 1863, Lincoln announced his Ten-Percent Plan of Reconstruction
         a. No role for blacks
         b. Leniency toward the South
      2. Freed blacks in New Orleans complained about the Ten-Percent Plan and found sympathy from Radical Republicans
      3. Wade-Davis Bill offered as an alternative plan
         a. Lincoln pocket-vetoed the plan
   D. Victory at Last
      1. Sherman marched to the sea in November 1864
      2. Thirteenth Amendment approved on January 31, 1865
      3. On April 3, 1865, Grant took Richmond
      4. Lee surrendered to Grant at Appomattox on April 9
      5. Lincoln fatally shot on April 12
   E. The War in American History
      1. The Civil War laid the foundation for modern America
      2. Poet Bret Harte gave blacks equality in death
         a. The work was to begin to give blacks equality in life

SUGGESTED DISCUSSION QUESTIONS

- Describe why the Civil War was both a modern war and a total war.
- Why wasn't the North more successful early on in the war when it had clear advantages over the South?
- Describe the various ways blacks aided in the war. Be sure to think about noncombative roles as well.
- Lincoln switched from using the term "union" to the term "nation." Discuss the significance of this shift in thinking.
- How does the Gettysburg Address express ideas of freedom and liberty? What purpose did Lincoln give the Civil War in that address?
- In the face of a significant manpower shortage, why was the South still so hesitant to use slaves as soldiers?
- Was Lincoln's reconstruction plan suitable considering the massive toll the Civil War took on American society?

SUPPLEMENTAL WEB AND VISUAL RESOURCES

The Civil War

www.pbs.org/civilwar/film/episode5.html

Documented by Ken Burns, Episode 5, "The Universe of Battle—1863," covers the battles of Gettysburg and Vicksburg and discusses the wartime participation of women and African-Americans.

www.films.com/Films_Home/item.cfm?s=1&bin=7055

This multimedia software was created by an Emmy Award–winning production team and documents the Civil War like no other.

Glory, a Hollywood film staring Denzel Washington, tells the story of the Massachusetts 54th Regiment. Produced by Tri-Star, 1989.

Robert E. Lee

www.civilwarhome.com/leebio.htm

This site highlights General Lee's contribution to the Civil War. More information can be found on other aspects of the Civil War as well.

Ulysses S. Grant

www.mscomm.com/~ulysses/page152.html

This site concentrates solely on Ulysses S. Grant. Many links are also available for further research.

The Emancipation Proclamation

usinfo.state.gov/usa/infousa/facts/democrac/24.htm

The Emancipation Proclamation is featured on this site with an introduction to the speech. This link is a part of a larger site dedicated to basic readings of U.S. democracy.

Jefferson Davis
www.civilwarhome.com/jdavisbio.htm
The extensive material on this Web site covers the role of Jefferson Davis during the war.

SUPPLEMENTAL PRINT RESOURCES

Bailey, Anne. "A Texas Cavalry Raid: Reaction to Black Soldiers and Contrabands." *Civil War History* 35, no. 2 (1989): 138–52.

Blight, David. *Race and Reunion: The Civil War in American Memory.* Cambridge: Harvard University Press, 2001.

Cimbala, Paul, and Randall Miller, eds., *An Uncommon Time: The Civil War and the Northern Home Front.* New York: Fordham University Press, 2002.

Faust, Drew Gilpin. *Mothers of Invention: Women of the Slaveholding South in the American Civil War.* Chapel Hill: University of North Carolina Press, 1996.

Harris, William H. *With Charity for All: Lincoln and the Restoration of the Union.* Louisville: University of Kentucky Press, 1997.

Reardon, Carol. *Pickett's Charge in History and Memory.* Chapel Hill: University of North Carolina Press, 1997.

TEST BANK

Matching

h	1. Ulysses S. Grant	a. 1864 Democratic presidential candidate
f	2. Jefferson Davis	b. challenged Lincoln for the 1864 Republican nomination
g	3. Thaddeus Stevens	c. marched through the South
a	4. George McClellan	d. teacher on the Sea Islands
i	5. Robert E. Lee	e. southern spy for the Union
j	6. Abraham Lincoln	f. president of the Confederacy
e	7. Elizabeth Van Lew	g. Radical Republican from Pennsylvania
b	8. John Fremont	h. practiced a war of attrition
d	9. Laura Towne	i. surrendered to General Grant
c	10. William T. Sherman	j. favored a Ten-Percent Plan for Reconstruction

h	1. Anaconda Plan	a. escaped slaves
j	2. Bull Run	b. deadliest battle of the war
d	3. Copperheads	c. Richmond

f	4. King Cotton Diplomacy	d. opponents of the war
b	5. Antietam	e. surrender of the Confederacy
i	6. Emancipation Proclamation	f. relied on British support
a	7. contrabands	g. Gettysburg
e	8. Appomattox	h. a naval blockade
g	9. Pickett's Charge	i. freed slaves
c	10. Confederate capital	j. spectators came with picnics to watch

Multiple Choice

1. The Union's manpower advantage over the Confederacy
   a. was short lived once the South used the slaves as troops
   *b. proved to be essential for the success of Grant's "war of attrition" strategy
   c. was a psychologically powerful tool over the South
   d. did not matter in determining the outcome of the war
   e. was achieved because the North had lower draft requirements than the South

2. What new technology used during the Civil War considerably changed the nature of combat?
   a. the musket
   b. the hot air balloon
   c. the machine gun
   *d. the rifle
   e. the tank

3. When war broke out, the North
   a. had very few accurate maps of the South
   b. had no national banking system
   c. had no tax system capable of raising substantial war funds
   d. had no national railroad gauge
   *e. all of the above

4. The Crittenden Compromise
   a. indicated that the North would draft blacks into the Army
   b. proposed the annexation of Cuba
   *c. affirmed that the Union had no intention of interfering with slavery
   d. emancipated slaves in Union-controlled territory
   e. set a code of ethics to be followed for prisoner of war camps

5. Lincoln stretched the reach of his constitutional powers by
   *a. twice suspending the writ of habeas corpus
   b. issuing the Gettysburg Address

c. switching to the term "nation" from the previously used "union"
d. allowing blacks to serve in the armed forces
e. all of the above

6. Jefferson Davis's strategy to win the war was based on
*a. cotton diplomacy
b. construction of a fortified wall along the Mason-Dixon line
c. slaves used as soldiers
d. constructing a navy to destroy the Union blockade
e. a war of attrition

7. At the First Battle of Bull Run
*a. spectators from the city came with picnics to watch
b. the Union won a smashing victory
c. the number of casualties taken that day exceeded any other battle of the war
d. the Confederates swept northward and captured Washington, D.C.
e. General Grant made a name for himself

8. In the first two years of the war, most of the fighting took place
a. in the western territories as Indians rose up to support the Confederacy
b. in the deep South, where Union forces won key victories at New Orleans and Shiloh
*c. in Virginia, where General Lee prevented General McClellan from advancing southward
d. in Washington, D.C., as both sides wrestled for control of the capitol
e. in the North, as the Union forces tried to expel the Confederates from Union territory

9. Which of the following best describes General George McClellan's character as a commander?
a. genius
b. always listened to Lincoln
c. too eager to take risks
*d. overestimated the enemy and stalled for time
e. a monster who ordered his men to commit atrocities against the enemy

10. At Antietam
a. General Lee was successful in pushing North
b. General McClellan surrendered his troops
*c. the nation sustained the worst casualties in its history
d. the war plan of the Confederacy worked well
e. Lincoln announced the Thirteenth Amendment

11. Lincoln was hesitant to support abolition early in the war because
a. he did not believe slaves could be productive American citizens
b. he owned slaves himself

*c. he did not want to lose the support of the slaveholding border states within the Union
d. he did not want to support the policies of the Radical Republicans
e. he promised during his 1860 campaign that he was against abolition

12. All of the following were factors that led Lincoln to conclude emancipation was necessary except
a. the North was losing the war
b. the British were sympathizing with the Confederacy
c. the North needed more manpower
*d. pressure from General Grant to do so
e. changing Northern public opinion that favored emancipation

13. The Emancipation Proclamation
a. freed all slaves
b. freed only those slaves in the loyal border states
c. freed only those slaves in states still in rebellion
*d. freed only those slaves in territory held by the Union army
e. none of the above

14. Black soldiers in the Union army
a. were treated worse than black sailors in the navy
b. found their service to be a liberating experience
c. had opportunities to serve in political office after the war
d. played a crucial role in defining the war's consequences
*e. all of the above

15. Union economic policies during the war
a. slowed down the North's economy
b. discouraged westward settlement
c. resulted in lower tariffs and reduced taxes
*d. increased the size and power of the federal government
e. prohibited women in the workforce

16. Copperheads were
*a. opponents of the war
b. supporters of copper coins
c. advocates for a national bank
d. proponents of the war
e. opponents of emancipation

17. General Sherman marched through the South to the sea
a. to meet up with Grant's army
b. to engage Lee in battle
*c. to demoralize the South's civilian population
d. to secure Richmond for the Union
e. to give freed slaves land

18. Which statement about the Confederacy is false?
    a. Jefferson Davis proved unable to communicate the war's meaning effectively to ordinary men and women
    b. The Confederate nation became far more centralized than the Old South had been
    c. Social change and internal turmoil engulfed much of the Confederacy
    d. The economy was in crisis and many families fell into poverty and debt
    *e. Because of a shortage of manpower, the South recruited and deployed black soldiers in the last year of the war

19. The "negro paradise" established by General Grant
    a. had blacks working for wages for whites
    b. was established on the Sea Islands
    *c. divided land among blacks to farm for themselves
    d. was adopted by Lincoln as part of his Reconstruction plan
    e. included a mule for every family

20. Lincoln's plan for Reconstruction can be best characterized as
    a. harsh
    b. moderate
    *c. lenient
    d. radical
    e. he did not have a plan

True or False

T 1. On both sides, the outbreak of war stirred powerful feelings of patriotism.

F 2. It was clear to most people from the beginning of the war that the war meant the end of slavery.

F 3. Overall, the casualties of the Civil War were approximately equivalent to American casualties taken during World War II.

F 4. The Union naval blockade was very effective early in the war.

T 5. Lincoln's primary purpose in raising troops to put down the southern rebellion was to restore the Union.

T 6. Due to Lincoln's announcement of the Emancipation Proclamation, Republicans suffered sharp reverses in the 1862 midterm elections.

T 7. The Emancipation Proclamation represented a turning point in Lincoln's own thinking.

F 8. Less than 50,000 blacks served in the Union army during the war.

T 9. Black soldiers in the Union army that were captured by the Confederacy faced sale into slavery or immediate execution.

T 10. Civil liberties were occasionally violated during the war.

F 11. Lincoln raised the money to pay for the war mostly through an income tax.

T 12. Women took to factory jobs and nursing during the war.

T 13. The provision of the draft law allowing individuals to provide a substitute soldier or buy their way out of the army caused widespread indignation.

F 14. King Cotton Diplomacy was intended to promote economic self-sufficiency in the South and force France to intervene on the side of the Confederacy.

F 15. Desertion was not a major problem in the Confederate army as it was in the Union army.

F 16. Major General George Pickett led a charge, aptly known as Pickett's Charge, during the Second Battle at Bull Run.

T 17. Republican presidential hopeful John Fremont ran on a campaign that called for the confiscation of the land of leading Confederates.

T 18. The Sea Island experiment demonstrated how ex-slaves could be gainfully employed, educated, and well provided for.

F 19. In Lincoln's Ten-Percent Plan, blacks played a predominate role in Reconstruction.

F 20. The Thirteenth Amendment, like the rest of the Constitution to that point, never mentioned the words "slave" or "slavery."

Short Answer

Identify and give the historical significance of each of the following terms, events, and people in a paragraph or two.

1. King Cotton Diplomacy
2. black soldiers
3. Antietam
4. Homestead Act
5. Gettysburg
6. Emancipation Proclamation
7. Bull Run
8. New York draft riots
9. Sea Island experiment
10. Reconstruction plans

Essay Questions

1. What did the Union soldiers believe they were fighting for? What did the Confederate soldiers believe they were fighting for?
2. What advantages did the South have? Why did they think victory would be theirs?
3. Describe Lincoln's leadership abilities. How important were they for victory? Compare Lincoln to the Confederate president, Jefferson Davis.
4. How did the war affect the economies of the North and of the South?
5. What strategy did General Grant adopt for a Union victory? Be sure to fully discuss why it was criticized and why it was destined to defeat the South.
6. Abraham Lincoln did not call upon 700,000 troops in 1861 to suppress the Confederate rebellion thinking that the nation was going to plunge into a total war. Describe the changes in Lincoln's thinking that led to a total war that was being fought for high ideals. How did it move from quelling an insurrection to a total war that redefined the meanings of freedom and liberty?
7. Using Lincoln's speech at Sanitary Fair in 1864 excerpted in *Voices of Freedom,* explain how Lincoln defined liberty. How does this speech reflect a change in his thinking from 1861?
8. Blacks eagerly signed up for service in the army and navy after the Emancipation Proclamation was issued. Describe the life of a black soldier. How did it differ from the experiences of black sailors? Overall, how important were black servicemen in the outcome of the war? Finally, discuss what fighting in the war meant to these men.
9. Frederick Douglass declared, "The work does not *end* with the abolition of slavery, but only *begins*." In a thoughtful essay, discuss what you foresee as the work that would need to be done to secure freedom and liberty for the ex-slaves. Is emancipation enough? Why or why not?

CHAPTER 15

"What Is Freedom?": Reconstruction, 1865–1877

This chapter concentrates on the history of Reconstruction. Opening with an explanation of Special Field Order 15 from General Sherman that set aside "40 acres and a mule" for the freedmen, the chapter explores what freedom meant to blacks and how white American society responded to emancipation. The meaning of freedom for blacks was many, and they relished the opportunity to express their liberation from slavery. Land ownership became a contentious issue as blacks were ultimately denied free access to land. Highlighting this controversy is *Voices of Freedom,* which features a petition from freedmen to Johnson in regard to land. Likewise, due to the devastation caused by the Civil War, many white farmers faced poverty as tenant farmers and sharecroppers. The politics of Reconstruction is explored next, viewing Lincoln's Ten-Percent Plan as moderate, Andrew Johnson's plan as too lenient, and the Radical Republicans' plan as groundbreaking. With Johnson's many presidential pardons to ex-Confederates and the South's implementation of Black Codes, the Republicans in Congress fought back with the Civil Rights Act of 1866, the Fourteenth Amendment, and the Military Reconstruction Act. Johnson resisted and was impeached by the House, but avoided being removed from office by the Senate. The Fifteenth Amendment finished the Radical Republicans' Reconstruction agenda, but split the feminist movement due to its failure to give the vote to women. The chapter then looks at how Reconstruction shaped southern politics as blacks held over 2,000 public offices. The white southerners, however, felt threatened by black suffrage and the Ku Klux Klan began a campaign of terror and violence. After the Klan was abolished through the efforts of President Grant, the South took matters into its own hands and began to "redeem" itself from perceived corruption, misgovernment, and northern and black control. Reconstruction ended in 1877, after a compromise was met between the Republicans and Democrats on the 1876 presidential election.

CHAPTER OUTLINE

I. "Sherman Land"

II. The Meaning of Freedom
  A. Blacks and the Meaning of Freedom
    1. African-Americans' understanding of freedom was shaped by their experience as slaves and observation of the free society around them
    2. Blacks relished the opportunity to demonstrate their liberation from the regulations, significant and trivial, associated with slavery
  B. The Black Family in Freedom
    1. The family was central to the post-Emancipation black community
    2. Freedom subtly altered relationships within the family
      a. Black women withdrew to their private sphere
  C. Church and School
    1. The rise of the independent black church, with Methodists and Baptists commanding the largest followings, redrew the religious map of the South
      a. Black ministers came to play a major role in politics
    2. Blacks of all ages flocked to the schools established by northern missionary societies, the Freedmen's Bureau, and groups of ex-slaves themselves
  D. Political Freedom
    1. The right to vote inevitably became central to the former slaves' desire for empowerment and equality
      a. Being denied suffrage meant "the stigma of inferiority"
    2. To demonstrate their patriotism, blacks throughout the South organized July 4th celebrations
  E. Land, Labor, and Freedom
    1. Former slaves' ideas of freedom were directly related to land ownership
      a. Many former slaves insisted that through their unpaid labor, they had acquired a right to the land
  F. Masters without Slaves
    1. The South's defeat was complete and demoralizing
      a. Planter families faced profound changes
    2. Most planters defined black freedom in the narrowest manner
      a. Freedom was defined as a privilege, not a right
  G. The Free Labor Vision
    1. The victorious Republican North tired to implement its own vision of freedom
      a. Free labor
    2. The Freedmen's Bureau was to establish a working free-labor system

H. The Freedmen's Bureau
   1. The task of the Bureau was daunting
   2. The Bureau's achievements in some areas, notably education and health care, were striking

I. Land and Labor
   1. Blacks wanted land of their own, not jobs on plantations
   2. President Andrew Johnson ordered nearly all land in federal hands returned to its former owners
   3. Because no land distribution took place, the vast majority of rural freed people remained poor and without property during Reconstruction

J. Toward a New South
   1. Sharecropping came to dominate the cotton South and much of the tobacco belt
   2. Sharecropping initially arose as a compromise between blacks' desire for land and planters' for labor discipline

K. The White Farmer
   1. Aftermath of the war hurt small white farmers
      a. Crop lien
   2. Both black and white farmers found themselves caught in the sharecropping and crop lien systems
      a. Every census from 1880 to 1940 counted more white than black sharecroppers

L. The Urban South
   1. Southern cities experienced remarkable growth after the Civil War
      a. Rise of a new middle class

III. The Making of Radical Reconstruction

A. Andrew Johnson
   1. Johnson identified himself as the champion of the "honest yeomen" and a foe of large planters
   2. Johnson lacked Lincoln's political skills and keen sense of public opinion
   3. Johnson believed that African-Americans had no role to play in Reconstruction

B. The Failure of Presidential Reconstruction
   1. Johnson's plan for Reconstruction offered pardons to the white southern elite
   2. Johnson's plan allowed the new state governments a free hand in managing local affairs

C. The Black Codes
   1. Southern governments began passing new laws that restricted the freedom of blacks
   2. These new laws violated free-labor principles and called forth a vigorous response from the Republican North

D. The Radical Republicans
    1. Radical Republicans called for the dissolution of Johnson's state governments and new ones established without "rebels" in power that gave blacks the right to vote
    2. The Radicals fully embraced the expanded powers of the federal government born of the Civil War
        a. Charles Summer
        b. Thaddeus Stevens
    3. Thaddeus Stevens's most cherished aim was to confiscate the land of disloyal planters and divide it among former slaves and northern migrants to the South
        a. His plan was too radical

E. The Origins of Civil Rights
    1. Most Republicans were moderates, not radicals
    2. Senator Lyman Trumbull of Illinois proposed two bills to modify Johnson's policy
        a. Extend the life of the Freedmen's Bureau
        b. Civil Rights Bill
    3. Johnson vetoed both bills
    4. Congress passed the Civil Rights Bill over his veto

F. The Fourteenth Amendment
    1. It placed in the Constitution the principle of citizenship for all persons born in the United States, and empowered the federal government to protect the rights of all Americans
        a. It did not provide for black suffrage
    2. The Fourteenth Amendment produced an intense division between the parties

G. The Reconstruction Act
    1. Johnson campaigned against the Fourteenth Amendment in the 1866 mid-term elections
    2. In March 1867, over Johnson's veto, Congress adopted the Reconstruction Act

H. Impeachment and the Election of Grant
    1. To demonstrate his dislike for the Tenure of Office Act, Johnson removed the secretary of war from office in 1868
    2. Johnson was impeached and the Senate fell one vote short to remove him from office
    3. Ulysses S. Grant won the 1868 presidential election

I. The Fifteenth Amendment
    1. Congress approved the Fifteenth Amendment in 1869
    2. Provided for black suffrage
        a. Had many loopholes
        b. Did not extend suffrage to women

J. The "Great Constitutional Revolution"
   1. The laws and amendments of Reconstruction reflected the intersection of two products of the Civil War era—a newly empowered national state and the idea of a national citizenry enjoying equality before the law
   2. Before the Civil War, American citizenship had been closely linked to race
      a. Naturalization Act of 1790
      b. *Dred Scott* decision of 1857
   3. The new amendments also transformed the relationship between the federal government and the states
K. The New Boundaries of Freedom
   1. That the United States was a "white man's government" had been a widespread belief before the Civil War
   2. Reconstruction Republicans' belief in universal rights also had its limits
      a. Asians still excluded from citizenship
L. The Rights of Women
   1. The destruction of slavery led feminists to search for ways to make the promise of free labor real for women
   2. Other feminists debated how to achieve "liberty for married women"
M. Feminists and Radicals
   1. Talk of woman suffrage and redesigning marriage found few sympathetic male listeners
   2. Feminists were divided over their support for the Fifteenth Amendment
      a. National Women Suffrage Association
      b. American Woman Suffrage Association
   3. Despite their limitations, the Fourteenth and Fifteenth Amendments and the Reconstruction Act of 1867 marked a radical departure in American and world history

IV. Radical Reconstruction in the South
   A. "The Tocsin of Freedom"
      1. Among the former slaves, the passage of the Reconstruction Act inspired an outburst of political organization
      2. These gatherings inspired direct action to remedy long-standing grievances
      3. The Union League aided blacks in the public sphere
      4. By 1870 the Union had been restored and southern states held Republican majorities
   B. The Black Officeholder
      1. Two thousand African-Americans occupied public offices during Reconstruction
         a. Fourteen elected to the House of Representatives
         b. Two elected to the Senate

2. The presence of black officeholders and their white allies made a real difference in southern life
3. Robert Smalls of South Carolina

C. Carpetbaggers and Scalawags
1. Carpetbaggers were northerners who often held political office in the South
2. Scalawags were white southern Republicans

D. Southern Republicans in Power
1. Established the South's first state-supported public schools
2. The new governments also pioneered in civil rights legislation
3. Republican governments also took steps to strengthen the position of rural laborers and promote the South's economic recovery
4. Every state during Reconstruction helped to finance railroad construction

V. The Overthrow of Reconstruction

A. Reconstruction's Opponents
1. Corruption did exist during Reconstruction, but it was confined to no race, region, or party
2. Opponents could not accept the idea of former slaves voting, holding office, and enjoying equality before the law

B. "A Reign of Terror"
1. Secret societies sprang up in the South with the aim of preventing blacks from voting and destroying the organization of the Republican Party
2. Ku Klux Klan organized in 1866
   a. It launched what one victim called a "reign of terror" against Republican leaders, black and white

C. The Challenge of Enforcement
1. Congress and President Grant put an end to the Ku Klux Klan by 1872

D. The Liberal Republicans
1. The North's commitment to Reconstruction waned during the 1870s
2. Some Republicans formed a new party called the Liberal Republicans
   a. Horace Greeley
3. Liberal Republicans believed that power in the South should be returned to the region's "natural leaders"

E. The North's Retreat
1. The Liberal attack on Reconstruction contributed to a resurgence of racism in the North
2. The 1873 depression also distracted the North from Reconstruction
3. The Supreme Court whittled away at the guarantees of black rights Congress had adopted

F. The Triumph of the Redeemers
   1. Redeemers claimed to have "redeemed" the white South from corruption, misgovernment, and northern and black control
      a. Violence was in broad daylight

G. The Disputed Election and Bargain of 1877
   1. The election between Rutherford B. Hayes and Samuel Tilden was very close
   2. Congress intervened
   3. Hayes won the election through a compromise
   4. Reconstruction ended in 1877
   5. Even while it lasted, however, Reconstruction revealed some to the tensions inherent in the nineteenth-century discussions of freedom

SUGGESTED DISCUSSION QUESTIONS

- There were many proposals for various land reforms. Describe the various plans, why they did not work, and the consequences of their failure. Discuss the petition to Andrew Johnson in *Voices of Freedom.*
- Describe Lincoln's plan for Reconstruction. How was his plan a reflection of his adherence to preserving the Union?
- What course did presidential Reconstruction take? How did the South respond?
- What did freedom mean to the blacks? How did they express their newfound freedom?
- What made the Radical Republicans "radical"?
- Discuss Charles Sumner's remark that rather than a threat to liberty, the federal government had become "the custodian of freedom."
- Why did Reconstruction come to an end in 1877?

SUPPLEMENTAL WEB AND VISUAL RESOURCES

Andrew Johnson

www.grolier.com/presidents/ea/bios/17pjhnsn.html

This site focuses on the American presidency in general but has a helpful biography on Andrew Johnson. Included are recommended readings and links to other material.

Fourteenth Amendment

www.grolier.com/presidents/ea/bios/17pjhnsn.html

The Fourteenth Amendment is well documented on this site with annotations at the bottom of the page.

Reconstruction Act

www.ncrepublic.org/recon3.html

This North Carolina American Republic Web site contains plenty of links to other relevant material concerning the Reconstruction Act.

Ku Klux Klan
www.spartacus.schoolnet.co.uk/USAkkk.htm
This is an excellent site that covers the history of the Ku Klux Klan.

Black Communities after the Civil War
www.films.com/Films_Home/item.cfm?s=1&bin=8346
This film concentrates on black communities after the Civil War and includes the increasing violence that occurred from the Ku Klux Klan.

SUPPLEMENTAL PRINT RESOURCES

Bond, James. *No Easy Walk to Freedom: Reconstruction and the Ratification of the Fourteenth Amendment.* Westport, CT: Praeger, 1997.

Brown, Elsa Barkley. "Negotiating and Transforming the Public Sphere: African American Political Life in the Transition from Slavery to Freedom. "*Public Culture* 7 (1994): 107–146.

Cimbala, Paul. *Under the Guardianship of the Nation: The Freedmen's Bureau and the Reconstruction of Georgia, 1865–1870.* Athens: University of Georgia Press, 1997.

Duncan, Russell. *Freedom's Shore: Tunis Campbell and the Georgia Freedmen.* Athens: University of Georgia Press, 1987.

Foner, Eric. *Nothing But Freedom: Emancipation and Its Legacy.* Baton Rouge: Louisiana State University Press, 1983.

McPherson, James. *Abraham Lincoln and the Second American Revolution.* New York: Oxford University Press, 1991.

TEST BANK

Matching

f	1. Thaddeus Stevens	a. secretary of war
c	2. Andrew Johnson	b. proposed the Civil Rights Bill of 1866
j	3. Charles Sumner	c. presidential Reconstruction
h	4. Rutherford B. Hayes	d. Liberal Republicans' presidential candidate
a	5. Edwin Stanton	e. first black Senator
i	6. Elizabeth Cady Stanton	f. Radical Republican congressman from Pennsylvania
b	7. Lyman Trumbull	g. Whiskey Ring

e	8. Hiram Revels	h. ended Reconstruction
g	9. Ulysses S. Grant	i. National Woman Suffrage Association
d	10. Horace Greeley	j. Radical Republican senator from Massachusetts

c	1. Special Field Order 15	a. restrictions placed on freed blacks in South
d	2. carpetbaggers	b. home rule
g	3. Howard University	c. "40 acres and a mule"
i	4. scalawags	d. Northerners who came to the South during Reconstruction
a	5. Black Codes	e. ended Reconstruction
j	6. Ten-Percent Plan	f. government agency that helped blacks in South
b	7. redeemers	g. black school in Washington, D.C
e	8. Compromise of 1877	h. terror organization
f	9. Freedmen's Bureau	i. white southern Republican
h	10. Ku Klux Klan	j. Lincoln's plan for Reconstruction

Multiple Choice

1. The Special Field Order 15 issued by General Sherman
   a. gave freed slaves the right to find their family members who had been sold away
   *b. set aside the Sea Islands and forty-acre tracts of land in South Carolina and Georgia for black families
   c. gave "40 acres and a mule" to blacks who wished to move to the unsettled American Southwest
   d. gave his army instructions to burn their way through the South to the coast
   e. established the Freedmen's Bureau to help blacks make the transition from slavery to freedom

2. Which of the following *best* describes the black response to the ending of the Civil War and the coming of freedom?
   a. Sensing the continued hatred of whites toward them, most blacks wished to move back to Africa
   b. Most blacks stayed with their old masters because they were not familiar with any other opportunities
   *c. Blacks adopted different ways of testing their freedom, including moving about, seeking kin, and rejecting older forms of deferential behavior
   d. Desiring better wages, most blacks moved to the northern cities to seek factory work

e. Most blacks were content working for wages and not owning their own land because they believed that they had not earned the right to just be given land from the government

3. With slavery dead, which black institution strengthened after the war?
   a. the free blacks' church
   b. the secret slave church
   c. the black family
   d. the free blacks' schools
   *e. all of the above

4. The Freedmen's Bureau's greatest achievements were in
   *a. education and health care
   b. legal representation and employment
   c. land redistribution and law enforcement
   d. prosecuting Confederates and rebuilding southern infrastructure
   e. suffrage for blacks and citizenship for blacks

5. Lincoln's plan for Reconstruction was based upon
   *a. ten percent of the 1860 electorate taking an oath of allegiance to the Union
   b. confiscating southern land and redistributing it to the ex-slaves under the slogan "40 acres and a mule."
   c. a military occupation of the South until the southern states wrote new constitutions guaranteeing black suffrage
   d. ratifying the Fourteenth Amendment
   e. presidential pardons for the former Confederate leadership so that they might regain office in Congress

6. Which statement about Andrew Johnson is false?
   a. Johnson identified himself as the champion of the "honest yeomen" and a foe of large planters
   *b. Johnson campaigned for the ratification of the Fourteenth Amendment, against his party's wishes
   c. Johnson lacked Lincoln's political skills and keen sense of public opinion
   d. Johnson believed that African-Americans had no role to play in Reconstruction
   e. Johnson's plan for Reconstruction offered pardons to the white southern elite

7. The "Black Codes" of the South
   a. declared black suffrage
   b. were a series of steps outlined by the Freedmen's Bureau to gain employment
   c. were codes of conduct that ex-slaves developed to demonstrate their Christianity and education

*d. resembled old slave codes and placed many restrictions upon ex-slaves' freedom
e. were denounced by President Johnson and ruled to be unconstitutional by the Supreme Court

8. The most ambitious, but least successful of the Radical Republicans' aims was
*a. land reform
b. black suffrage
c. federal protection of civil rights
d. public education
e. reunification of the Union

9. Andrew Johnson vetoed the 1866 Civil Rights Act because
a. he believed that the protection of civil rights was a federal responsibility, not one for the states
b. it did not include suffrage for blacks, something he thought was needed
*c. he did not believe that blacks deserved the rights of citizenship
d. he was angry at Congress and refused to pass any of its legislation
e. none of the above

10. The Fourteenth Amendment
a. abolished slavery
b. guaranteed that suffrage could not be denied on account of race
c. severely punished the ex-Confederates
d. established the Freedmen's Bureau
*e. declared that anyone born or naturalized in the United States was a citizen

11. The Naturalization Act of 1790 and the *Dred Scott* decision both illustrate that prior to the Civil War, citizenship had been closely linked to
*a. race
b. property ownership
c. gender
d. freedom
e. birthplace

12. The passage of the Fifteenth Amendment
a. split the feminist movement into two major organizations
b. had been bitterly opposed by the Democratic Party
c. marked the end of the American Antislavery Society, as its work was now complete
d. left many loopholes for the South to disfranchise blacks
*e. all of the above

13. Elizabeth Cady Stanton and Susan B. Anthony founded the
*a. National Woman Suffrage Association

b. Women's Christian Temperance Union
c. first Settlement House
d. Equal Rights Association
e. Fifteenth Amendment Advocacy Society

14. Hiram Revels and Blanche Bruce were the first two black
 a. congressmen
 b. governors
 c. mayors
 *d. senators
 e. federal judges

15. Carpetbaggers and scalawags
 a. were out for personal gain, taking advantage of Reconstruction
 b. were Democrats who wanted to help the blacks in the South
 c. were largely ignored and unsuccessful in the South
 *d. were northern and southern Republicans who sought political office in the South
 e. were terror groups who advocated violence towards blacks in the South

16. What was not an accomplishment of the Republicans in the South during Reconstruction?
 a. state-supported public schools
 *b. land reform
 c. pioneering civil rights legislation
 d. finance of railroad construction in the region
 e. tax incentives to attract northern manufacturers to invest in the region

17. Liberal Republicans believed that
 *a. power in the South should be returned to the region's "natural leaders"
 b. it was the responsibility of the federal government to continue assisting blacks
 c. President Grant was a brilliant politician
 d. Thaddeus Stevens would be their best presidential hope in 1876
 e. Congress had to stay committed to the Reconstruction cause

18. Who claimed to have converted the white South from corruption, misgovernment, and northern and black control?
 a. Republicans
 b. carpetbaggers
 *c. redeemers
 d. scalawags
 e. Ku Klux Klan

19. The election of 1876
 a. was won by Rutherford B. Hayes by a landslide
 b. was finally decided by the Supreme Court

c. marked the final stage of Reconstruction, which ended in 1880
*d. was close and tainted by claims of fraud in Florida, South Carolina, and Louisiana
e. was won by Ulysses S. Grant by a narrow count

20. The Bargain of 1877
a. allowed Samuel Tilden to become president
*b. ended Reconstruction
c. marked a compromise between Radical and Liberal Republicans
d. called for the passage of the Fifteenth Amendment
e. was made by Grant to end the Whiskey Ring

True or False

T 1. During Reconstruction black ministers played a major role in politics, holding some 250 public offices.

T 2. The Civil War was devastating to the South, which lost nearly one-fifth of its adult white male population.

F 3. Because of land redistribution, the vast majority of rural freed people prospered during Reconstruction.

F 4. By the mid-1870s, white farmers were cultivating as much as 80 percent of the South's cotton crop.

T 5. By and large, white voters in the South returned prominent Confederates and members of the old elite to power during presidential Reconstruction.

F 6. Compared to the rest of world history, the rebels of the defeated Confederacy were treated very harshly.

T 7. Thaddeus Stevens's most cherished aim was to confiscate the land of disloyal planters and divide it among former slaves and northern migrants to the South.

T 8. The Civil Rights Act of 1866 became the first major law in American history to be passed over a presidential veto.

F 9. The Senate, following the House's impeachment, removed Andrew Johnson from office.

F 10. With the passage of the Fourteenth Amendment, all peoples born in the United States were automatically citizens, including the Chinese, who had previously been barred from citizenship.

T 11. Lucy Stone favored the Fifteenth Amendment and established the American Woman Suffrage Association.

F 12. When the Union was restored by 1870, the southern states held Democratic majorities.

F 13. Black suffrage made little difference in the South as very few blacks ran for public office.

F 14. Since Reconstruction, both the House of Representatives and the Senate have had at least one black member.

T 15. White southern Democrats considered scalawags traitors to both their party and race.

T 16. While Republicans were in power in the South, they established the region's first state-supported public schools.

T 17. Opponents of Radical Reconstruction could not accept the idea of former slaves voting, holding office, and enjoying equality before the law.

F 18. The Ku Klux Klan was an organization of the lower classes of the South—those who felt left out of white society.

T 19. In Mississippi, in 1875, white rifle clubs drilled in public and openly assaulted and murdered Republicans.

F 20. The 1873 depression strengthened the North's resolve to ensure the success of Reconstruction since the depression really hurt the South's farmers, highlighting the need for reform in the region.

Short Answer

Identify and give the historical significance of each of the following terms, events, and people in a paragraph or two.

1. Fourteenth Amendment
2. Ku Klux Klan
3. Wade-Davis Bill
4. Andrew Johnson
5. sharecropping
6. Radical Republicans
7. Black Codes
8. Freedmen's Bureau
9. Fifteenth Amendment
10. redeemers

Essay Questions

1. What did "freedom" mean for the ex-slaves? Be sure to address economic opportunities, gender roles, religious independence, and family security.
2. Why did Radical Republicans believe that Andrew Johnson would support their agenda? Why was Johnson ultimately unable to lend his support to the Civil Rights Act of 1866 or the Fourteenth Amendment?

3. For whites, freedom, no matter how defined, was a given, a birthright to be defended. For African-Americans, it was an open-ended process, a transformation of every aspect of their lives and of the society and culture that had sustained slavery in the first place. Defend this statement.
4. Explain how wartime devastation set in motion a train of events that permanently altered the white yeomanry's independent way of life, leading to what they considered a loss of freedom.
5. Reconstruction witnessed profound changes in the lives of southerners, black and white, rich and poor. Explain the various ways that the lives of these groups were changed. How were the changes for the better or worse?
6. Stating that he "lived among men, not among angels," Thaddeus Stevens recognized that the Fourteenth Amendment was not perfect. Explain the strengths and weaknesses of the Fourteenth Amendment. What liberties and freedoms does it extend? Describe how it gave more power to the federal government at the expense of the states.
7. What faults did the Republicans see with presidential Reconstruction? How did they propose to rectify those deficiencies? Be sure to distinguish moderate Republicans from Radical Republicans in your answer.
8. Who were the redeemers, what did they want, and what were their methods? How did the redeemers feel that their freedom was being threatened? Conclude your essay with a comment on how you think the federal government should have responded to the redeemers.
9. Analyze whether or not "40 acres and a mule" would have made a difference in the outcome of Reconstruction.
10. Fully discuss the successes and failures of Reconstruction. Be sure to explain how freedom was expanded or constricted for various groups of people.